POEMS

POEMS

JAMES REANEY

EDITED BY GERMAINE WARKENTIN

EDITORIAL

ISBN O-88770-708-4

Original Edition
First Printing

new press
Order Department
553 Richmond Street West
Toronto 133, Ontario

Manufactured in Canada

CONTENTS

INTRODUCTION

In the last lines of James Reaney's poem "The Canadian" (1949), the speaker is shut up in the wintry parlour of an Ontario farmhouse, staring at the scene before—or perhaps inside—him:

> So I long in this dark parlour,
> Dull green, brown and maroon,
> The colour of starling feathers,
> This stuffy, dingy room.
> These dreams of tropical weathers!
> My grim grandfather!
> The Fathers of Confederation!
> These windows embossed
> With a mocking white imitation
> Of what I wish for, in frost.

This is the psychic setting of Reaney's earliest poetry: the farmhouse scene all too intimately known, the frustration of its inmate, and the icy paradigm of art taunting him from the windowpane. But the lines were written even as the poet was shedding this sense of impoverishment. He had begun to understand that if he were in command of the art represented by the frost's cartoon, he could speak to the farmhouse world 'in tongues', and help it see itself at last, as Bible Sal does so ecstatically in his play *Colours in the Dark*.

Reaney's first book of poems, *The Red Heart*, was published in 1949, the year in which "The Canadian" was written. Its inventiveness, super-heated aestheticism, and wryness astonished readers of the new poet, and Louis Dudek, later to become a hostile critic of Reaney, saw in it a fresh beginning for Canadian poetry. Nine years elapsed before Reaney produced his second major work. This was *A Suit of Nettles* (1958), a long poem which baffled the audience of *The Red Heart*. Inventiveness now took the form of a virtuoso display of traditional metrical techniques, aestheticism had given way to passionate social satire in the antique genre of the pastoral, and wryness to a complex, multi-layered satirical gusto. Since that time Reaney has produced two smaller books, the idyllic *Twelve Letters to a Small Town* (1962) and the innocent, mordant, *The Dance of Death at London Ontario* (1963). He has issued nineteen numbers of an evangelical 'little' magazine, *Alphabet*, and has written a series of highly experimental dramas, culminating in the yet-to-be-produced *Donnelly* (1971). He is also a musician, painter, and printer, the best interpreter of his own *One-Man Masque*, and before all else, a committed teacher. His lyrics, critical articles, radio collages and plays have made Reaney a major figure, but perhaps because he has moved so fast, this is the first comprehensive collection of his poems to be published.

Reaney is an academic poet who has made clear his disdain for the "Wordsworth High Schools and T.S. Eliot Colleges" of his own country, and a nationalist in poetry who moves as easily in the company of Byron and Blake as that of Isabella Valancy Crawford and Irving Layton. An advocate of Northrop Frye's view that literature is made out of other literature, he has nevertheless devoted himself to exploring the relationship between the 'documents' of our human experience and the 'myths' that shape literary experience. Many of his poems deal with the humblest aspects of rural and small-town life, yet he can encompass the forty-three counties of Ontario in the forty-three fields of a Perth County farm, and all of human joy and dread in the life of the geese who live in them. These paradoxes are merely the diverse expressions of a central purpose of uncommon firmness. Writing to composer John Beckwith of a mutual project, he once said:

> The idea behind the whole 3 parts is that you see the whole world in a local grain of sand . . . The big legend about Canada is that it was once covered with a glacier—in the third part this glacier returns as a snowflake.
> I want the last part to be about the very few symbolic things I'd put in a box if Canada was to blow up.

The passage reminds us of the stress in Reaney's poetry on powerful images, the symbolic things of a rich imagination. There is a single structural principle common to all Reaney's creative thought, whether in poetry, drama, critical writing, or teaching. He is always preoccupied with a process of transformation or translation, in which the identity of seemingly unlike things is unexpectedly revealed and they are transformed from the voiceless chaos of human experience into the eloquence of metaphor. In *Colours in the Dark*, the pedant Dr. Button rages at his students, "A flower is not like a star! Nothing is like . . . anything else. You've got to get over thinking things are like other things," only to be floored by Bible Sal's triumphant flow of ancient Babylonian. Most often this 'translation', or discovering of likenesses, takes the form of the finding of what is lost: either the protagonist finds himself, or some humble daily object ("plate cup knife fork spoon and jug") takes on a kind of universal eloquence, or the poet (and with him the society to whom he speaks) is found. The longing for this is present even in his earliest poetry.

Between *The Red Heart* and *Donnelly* stretches a body of work large, practical, mischievous, and visionary. Reaney's habit is to work on poems for many years, sometimes revising them so much they become new works (compare, for example, "The Morning Dew" with its later version, "The Alphabet"). He often cannibalizes early poems to make later ones, sometimes altering them, sometimes not. The result is that his poems and plays form a thistly mass of common material that sometimes acquires final shape only from the impetus of publication. Despite this, we can see in his work a succession of influences: rural Ontario, the demands of writing for music, the alien scene of the prairies, the criticism of Northrop Frye, and the problems of writing for the stage. From this emerges a portrait of the growth of a conscious artist, one who commands an increasingly flexible poetic instrument, and at the same time discovers and contains an increasingly spacious concept of human experience.

The shape in which Reaney describes his own development is a biographical one, and can be seen in the play *Colours in the Dark* (1967), which is actually a kind of 'collected poems' as well as being a history of his self-discovery. Rehearsed in the auditorium of the high school the poet himself attended, and presented at the Stratford Festival, the play was intended to draw both poet and audience to that 'home place' in the human spirit towards which all Reaney's poetry moves. Born near Stratford in 1926, to a family evangelical in religion and of mixed Scottish, Irish and German origin, Reaney still retains at the centre of his poetic world the farm on which he was born. Part of the same scene is the intricate relationships of the extended family in which he is still intensely involved. Of all the images that his essentially symbolist poetic dwells on, the most recurrent are the farm terrain (seen both as fruitful orchard and neglected garden) and the true and false parents that surround the 'lost children' of his poems and dramas. As Reaney has developed as a poet, these images have been used in different ways: in poems like "Romaninth but Quakereleventh" they are rendered with detachment but great energy, while in *The Red Heart* poems, detachment becomes disillusion and the same scene takes on a demonic quality. Suddenly purified and pastoral in the poems of the early fifties, the farm scene changes yet again in recent years as Reaney has learned how to draw from it a grammar of images that can be used to render both dread and joy, which are for him the basic elements of all human experience.

At the University of Toronto, Reaney belonged to a vigorous literary group which briefly found expression in Paul Arthur's historic 'little' magazine, *Here and Now,* and to which he has continued to address himself over the years. At University College were Reaney, critic Robert Weaver, and poet Colleen Thibaudeau (who married Reaney in 1950), and at Victoria College a group of enthusiastic students who had collected around the critic Northrop Frye. Other friends included John Beckwith, who has composed music for several Reaney works, and his wife Pamela Terry, who was to direct Reaney's first plays. Reaney took little interest in Frye's theories until his last year at college, but he and his friends at Victoria co-operated in many projects, including one for an artistic group whose members would live together and publish a magazine called *Yonge Street* (streetcar transfers hand-pasted on the cover) as the expression of their communal spirit. *The Red Heart* (with many previously published poems revised, and in an arrangement made by Colleen Thibaudeau and Sybil Hutchinson) appeared just before Christmas, 1949, when Reaney had left for a teaching position in Manitoba.

The effect which *The Red Heart* had on its audience seems to be the one aimed at in an early poem, "A Table of Contents," still in manuscript:

> I wish my poetry to be
> A crowd of long ladies

Wandering through a paginated mist
Who are made of brambles
Laid horizontally
On top of each other
Each bramble
Stuck with many a strange
Plum and pear
Bur and Toad-eye.

I believe that poetry
Is the sound
Of the wound
With its red mouth
Speaking to itself.

The lyrics evoke a Perth County childhood and manhood, in images suffused with a longing that they should be perfect and complete, and the embittered and rather indulgent conviction that they are emblems of destruction. An early friend maintains that Reaney was preoccupied with problems of form at this time, and the structural weaknesses of certain *Red Heart* poems bear this out. Interestingly, though it was easier for him to approach a poetic problem through images rather than through structure, Reaney by no means found the first form of a poem arising from a particular image or combination of images. An image might be the end result, but often in the draft poems, where the image is still being born or has not yet emerged, he begins with the *voice*, with sound, with words repeated for their musical effect, or with exhortations like "Huzza!" (This habit can be seen shaping the character of an entire poem in the later "Doomsday, or the Red Headed Woodpecker.") An important modern influence on his sense of voice and its relation to versification was Edith Sitwell, as an early essay (*The Undergrad*, March, 1948) suggests.

Characteristically, his interest in Sitwell went well beyond the formal and technical to take in the whole range of her work, including the late religious poetry. And *The Red Heart* itself does not indicate Reaney's own range at this time. Certain poems in the serene *Twelve Letters to a Small Town* (1962) were already beginning to take their first form, and they recur in various states in Reaney's papers until they were hurried together for a radio performance in 1961, and publication the next year. Similarly, the early notebooks show a variety of preoccupations. The most important of these is a curiosity about the Canada outside Stratford. "A long poem on the Rebellion, 15 parts," says one note; another, "investigate the man who wrote O Canada." "A Novel about the Canadian Pacific" is projected, and in several places there appears the wretched figure of Tecumseh, to whom Reaney has since returned in fascination. The poems of *The Red Heart*, then, represent what was the dominant mode in Reaney's 'bizarre period', but not its only one. To the disapproval of contemporary reviewers, some early lyrics were revised before they were included in *The Red Heart*. The poet's aim was significant: he wanted to make them more accessible to his neighbours in Stratford.

The long poem "The Dead Rainbow" shows that by 1948 Reaney wanted to turn the motive power of the images and sound-patterns he was using into the extended matter of a serious poem. "The Dead Rainbow" is brutally excessive in its effect, but the lasting impression it leaves comes not merely from its elaborate despair, but from the struggle to control such a vision by means that were simply inadequate to the task. Several poems still in manuscript (one a calendar poem that presages the form of *A Suit of Nettles*) show how novel it was for him to work out the structure of a large poem that had to have several phases. It was at this time that he began to digest Frye's work, perhaps because its spaciousness of concept answered his need for formal and spiritual scope. In the first editorial of *Alphabet* (1960), Reaney wrote of the period when he was about to leave for the decade which he spent in Manitoba:

> I can remember about twelve years ago at Toronto feeling the final clutch of the so-called scientific world. Metaphors seemed lies. Poetry seemed to have no use at all. The moon looked enchanting through the trees on Charles Street, but the enchantment was really nothing but an illusion of clouds and fantasy covering up a hideous pock-marked spherical desert. When I told this part of my problem to a friend, whose work appears in this issue, he showed me a passage from *The Marriage of Heaven and Hell* which had the effect of starting me back to the belief I had held as a young child that metaphor is reality. Those were the months when young men and women sat up all night reading *Fearful Symmetry* which had just come out.

The friend was Richard Stingle, and his article "To Harpooneers" in the same issue of *Alphabet* is, after Reaney's own critical writings, by far the best guide to the activities of the so-called 'mythopoeic poets' who have gathered around Frye. Stingle reminds us that their central point of agreement is *not* love of classical myth and literary convention for their own sake, but belief in the power of the mind, lost in a sea of dread, to create the island of joyous order which it is their nature as men to desire. Writes Stingle:

> The fundamental assumption of the myth-making consciousness is the ascendancy of the creative human forms over non-human ones, of form over chaos, of life over death. *Human creativity does not project an illusion, as Marx would have it, but gives us the power to see in Nature a human shape.*

Reaney's commitment to the academy, both as poet and teacher, has to be understood in the light of this statement. The mythopoeic poets are not afraid of convention, because as craftsmen they consider it their business to master and use it. They reach out gregariously to the literary figures of the past because they see them as fellow explorers of the kind of creative act they are engaged in. Indeed, Reaney has contended that an academic poet is not a university person, but simply

one who understands how to use literary tradition to beget new poetry.
In a sense, no human is without this begetting power, as the poem "The
Baby" suggests. From his mother's womb, the baby tells us:

> And the darkness gave me
> > Two boneless wands or swords;
> I knew not their meaning then
> > Whether traps or rewards.
>
> One was the vorpal phallus
> > Filled with jostling army,
> Henhouse and palace
> > Street crowds and history.
>
> Two was the magic tongue
> > Stuffed with names and numbers,
> The string of song
> > The waker from fallen slumbers.

More than anyone else, Reaney has recognized the profound moral
and social centre of Frye's theory. The "vorpal phallus," capable of
begetting "jostling army . . . street crowds and history" is part of the
same human as the "magic tongue . . . waker from fallen slumbers."
Frye's vision, which he acknowledges originated in his studies of Blake,
is of a universe made completely intelligible. It is one which we can live
in contentedly because we have possessed it with our minds and it can
never henceforth be lost to us. This solution to the problem of the
relationship of poetic and social vision has not appealed to rationalist
critics. But for Reaney and his associates the distinction between
rational and irrational is fallacious. For them, the rational is something
man *achieves* as he literally makes the world around him by taking it
into his own understanding. The failure to do so brings dread and
alienation; success on the other hand brings a joy which is not merely
personal, but civic as well.

The first important expression of the new turn taken by Reaney's
poetry after "The Dead Rainbow" was the rural chamber-opera
Night-Blooming Cereus, the libretto of which he completed for John
Beckwith in 1953. "The eye looks at, beholds the star, the bright star
longs to be the eye," sings his village recluse, Mrs. Brown, as she, the
local telephone operator, a gardener friend, two unhappy young people,
and Mrs. Brown's lost grand-daughter discover the way to build the
kingdom of heaven in the tiny village of Shakespeare, Ontario.
Night-Blooming Cereus shows the first extended use of Reaney's
characteristic theme of the finding of what is lost, and it is here also
that the Biblical imagery of all his later work begins to appear. (Reaney
uses the Bible rather as a poet of the Renaissance might use classical
mythology, not with literal conviction, though his poetry is religious in
another sense, but as a source book of metaphor; its theological and
literary coherence provide him with a model of the universe at its most
joyously intelligible.) And it was in working on *Night-Blooming Cereus*
that Reaney encountered the technical problems which led to the
writing of *A Suit of Nettles*. As he wrote in "An Evening with Babble

and Doodle" (*Canadian Literature*, 12, Spring 1962), his poetic affairs were "in some disarray" at this transitional point in his career, and he was stunned by the technical problems posed by writing singable verse. It was here that he began to face up to the technical problems of his craft which were partly forecast in "The Dead Rainbow."

At the same time, Reaney—who has never travelled much—had been wrenched for the first time from the Ontario environment which had nurtured him, and thrust into the puzzle of the prairies. He has said that a poet who wants to escape the provincialism of Canada has two options open to him: education and exile. As an academic, he unhesitatingly accepts the way of education: "anything that helps you to read better surely ends up helping you to write better." But he also took the road of exile—to Winnipeg—and characteristically turned it into the shaping experience of his middle years. At first violently homesick, he began to cultivate his inner landscape. Then, bicycling and on long walks, he began to teach himself to 'read' an exterior landscape very different from the one he had always known. At the same time as he was learning what he has repeatedly asserted since then, that "the feeling of place is a power within us," he was also discovering the "rich set of 'things' past" that the haunting Red River scene presents to those who look for it. It was this experience that seems to have confirmed his sympathy with Frye's work, at the same time that it forged a strong connection between Reaney the mythopoeic poet and Reaney the national poet. By 'making human', that is, coming to understand, the Red River plain, he was fostering in himself the capacity to 'make real' Canada itself. The first expression this took was *A Suit of Nettles*, in which he created a satirical vision of Canada that comprehends the most intimate experiences of love, birth, and death, as well as the larger question of how these experiences, seen in the mass, take the form of "all history with its gaudy banners."

A Suit of Nettles is first of all a prolonged literary allusion, and one somewhat recondite to non-academics: its model is *The Shepherd's Calendar* of the Elizabethan poet Edmund Spenser, and its convention that of the pastoral poem, in which the young poet traditionally trains himself to write before he settles down to the epic task of interpreting his people to themselves. (Its background and complexities have been very well dealt with by Alvin Lee in his study *James Reaney*, 1968.) The characters of *A Suit of Nettles*, however, are not shepherds but farm-yard geese, and the purpose of the poem, in continuance of the agricultural metaphor, is an avowedly social one: to "beat fertility into a sterile land." But though the poem is fiendishly difficult, Reaney does not exclude his readers by talking over their heads or making fun of them. In the life and death of his learned geese he shows us our own life and death, and in his contempt for the birth-control ladies of "May" or the awful Scrutumnus of "August," calls up our buried desire to give life rather than despair of it, to make the world intelligible rather than submit to its apparent disorder. As he says at the beginning of "The Ferris Wheel" ("September"), "when you're on it you don't notice this phenomenon, but by that time you're a clown enjoying your pastime: right now we are learneds and we are enjoying the puzzle of the ferris wheel." The form of the poem, as Ross Woodman has suggested, likewise insists that we step back and contemplate the puzzle of Canada in one manic, yet completely integrated image. Notwithstanding Reaney's charm, the effect is somewhat challenging, and when *A Suit of Nettles* appeared it was diversely greeted as the most advanced poem yet written in Canada, and as one of the most disappointing from a poet of major promise for some time.

Written in three summers of intense concentration, between 1953 and 1956, *A Suit of Nettles* was approached as a formal task of self-education in the poet's craft; its title floats in search of a concept through the early notebooks, but in contrast with most of Reaney's other work, there are no drafts of earlier versions. It is a virtuoso exploration of the metrical resources a poet should command in order to achieve certain effects, and in it Reaney at last learned to control the distinctive poetic voice that makes possible the powerful symbolic and metrical economy of such lyrics as "The Ghost," "The Lost Child," and "Jordan." In *A Suit of Nettles* the large structural ambition of "The Dead Rainbow" finds at last a perfected poetic language which can be used for any purpose the poet conceives, whether that of the drunken preacher's sermon of the "September" eclogue:

> Lo, it was the last supper, I leader from gutter
> Tell you tall and short tinkery folks gathered.
> What did those white souls eat while their lord talked:
> I don't know indeed I don't, maybe sandwiches.
> And He said haughtily head up to the twelve,
> 'I'll ask you assafoetidae again I will,
> Isn't there one, one disciple with the spunk to betray me?'

or Valancy's song in the bardic contest of "April":

> *Your limbs are the rivers of Eden.*
> From the dead we see you return and arise,
> Fair girl, lost daughter:
> The swallows stream through the skies,
> Down dipping water,
> Skimming ground, and from chimney's foul dusk
> Their cousins the swifts tumble up as the tusk
> Of roar day
> In bright May
> Scatters them gliding from darkness to sun-cusp.

When Reaney returned to Toronto in 1956 to work on his doctorate under Frye, it was not to the author of *Fearful Symmetry*, but to the literary taxonomist of the *Anatomy of Criticism*, Frye's attempt to describe synoptically the shape of that literary experience he has so influentially contended is made out of other literary experience. The new book drew Reaney's attention to the problems of 'reading' in a much larger context than that of reading a landscape. He began to be preoccupied with reading the shapes created by the mind, particularly as they were expressed in the structure of words which is literature. A series of poems began to develop in an arrangement modelled on Bach's *Well-Tempered Clavier*: they were attempts to render the 'modes' of which **Frye** writes in a set of exemplary literary exercises. This programme was abandoned, though some of the resulting poems can be seen in "A Sequence in Four Keys." Nevertheless, Reaney began to think that if the mind worked in this way, one could develop a virtual iconography of the imagination, an alphabet of images which would disclose the relationship between "the verbal universe which hovers over the seedbed of the so-called real and natural world picking out this or that event for admission into its world of literary forms" and the seedbed itself. This concept was at the root of the magazine *Alphabet*, with its investigation of individual myths, and its recurrent juxtaposition of 'myth' or literary shape with 'document' or human experience. In an important article in *Canadian Art* (Sept.-Oct. 1965) Reaney suggests how it underlay his later work with emblems.

As the poem "Alphabet" shows, this programme is no abstract literary game but leads to a vision essentially social. There the calling up of the letters of the alphabet is also the calling up of the names of the stores that build the wall of the New Jerusalem. It is this Biblical vision of social perfection that underlies the activism of the poetry and plays written since Reaney returned to Ontario (to London, not far from Stratford) in 1960. As the long poem *A Message to Winnipeg* suggests, Reaney sees in the society about him a city burning down. Yet he is also possessed with the belief that ordinary men can extinguish the conflagration by regaining power over their own imaginations, and consequently the world around them. The radio collage *The Line Up and Down* (which now exists only as a musical score) is preoccupied with this problem. Reaney leads the listener along downtown Yonge Street in Toronto, where man has seemingly anaesthetized himself out of despair, yet where the secret harmony of fruit in a store-front display hints of other voices murmuring under the shabbiness of city life. The listener is then taken up Yonge Street on a journey back through history, to a building which next to Reaney's childhood farmhouse is the most important in his work: David Willson's beautiful temple at Sharon, Ontario. Sharon Temple is a pioneer church unlike any other; built on a four-square, numerologically organized floor-plan, it is Reaney's symbol of what he feels is most needed in Canada: the need to build entirely native things unlike those in Europe, but on a plan so universal that they will not cut us off from other humans in provincial isolation, but bring us into communion with them. "Build David Willson's temple again?" asks one of the voices in his collage, "but it's still standing!" Replies the other gently, "the new one will be different from the old, though the pattern will be the same."

This is why Reaney's latest work presses on its audience the necessity of undertaking for themselves the process of self-illumination outlined in *Colours in the Dark*. Since the period of the 'clavier' poems, his poetry has diversified in a number of ways in order to do this, and he has actually been more occupied with drama than with verse. The mature Reaney is an artist capable of bringing us to a recognition of both the fundamental human states of joy and dread. The tranquillity of *Twelve Letters to a Small Town* does not give way to the antic grimness of *The Dance of Death at London Ontario*, but is co-existent with it, as is the wondering child's voice of "The Young Traveller" with the angular, non-human one of the split-tongued starling. The many bird poems (there are others still in manuscript) show how Reaney has persisted in devoting his prodigious technique to describing the total shape of human experience. The birds are the prime instances in his poetry of the power of metaphor; they give us visions into all kinds of states of being, from that of the sparrow in his urine-soaked gutter to the yellow-bellied sapsucker who signifies for the speaker the Bible-like unity of all existence. Most important of the poet's birds is the killdeer; "everything I love about my native province" says Reaney, "is summed up in the killdeer's cry." In the poem "The Killdeer" the bird becomes an emblem of the coherence and finality of Revelation itself:

> There was nothing left but the killdeer,
> He skated the cold spring air
> Over the old pasture, the line of elms,
> The Easter farmhouse, I there

> Heard his cry
> And saw all vanish into him:
> All time, all Space, all Bible
> Into that giant stormy die.

One-Man Masque begins with the masquer asking the audience the question "How does one live?" and answering,

> Oh, you mix up time and space. Space? Space is when you reach into your head for the red ball you see there and it isn't there! It's out there--somewhere! Put on your eyes--you're blind without them. Time? Time is when you see a thing out there and later on you don't see it out there. But you can only see it in here. So there's been a thing called time come along.

The puzzle of time and space, and the persistent question of how what is "out there" (in the world) gets "in here" (into the imagination) shapes Reaney's most recent work, the emblem poems, most of his dramas, and his teaching at the University of Western Ontario. All of these are designed to induce in his audience that act of the imagination which will make them reach from one to the other. His emblem poems come from a tradition four centuries old which was designed precisely for this teaching function. His dramas do the same through their emphasis on transparently improvised, audience-involving illusions. His teaching, which is presently focussed on Canadian literature, aims to make the student aware that the academy is not a dead and imprisoning institution, but is something inside him that he can learn to tend and use. The "torn orchardry" of Reaney's first version of "The School Globe" has given way to the orchard of his late emblem, to the orchard which he has maintained is inside us all. It is learning to tend this orchard that for Reaney has turned the still pond of "The Upper Canadian" into the flowing stream of "To the Avon River above Stratford, Canada," the wintry landscape in which the lost child hides into one that can be made anew:

I push the shore and kingdom to you,
O winter walk with seedpod ditch:
I touch them to the floating child
And lo! Cities and gardens, shepherds and smiths.

Victoria College   Germaine Warkentin
August, 1972

Acknowledgements

My foremost debt is to James Reaney himself, who made his files freely available, and entrusted to me the choosing of the poems to be included. Many of his friends and associates have also helped with advice and encouragement. In particular, I would like to thank Reaney's wife, Colleen Thibaudeau, for her perceptive comments on the project. John Beckwith, Sybil Hutchinson, and Jay Macpherson kindly made important material available. Margaret Gayfer, Richard Stingle, Pamela Terry, and Robert Weaver took special pains to recall information which might help. Among my own colleagues, Eleanor Cook helped me to see Reaney's poetry from the point of view of the teacher, and David Sinclair provided several texts. I am grateful also to the Canadian Music Centre for allowing me to work in its archive.

The first chapter of the emblem poems first appeared in *Poetry* (Chicago).

The drawing for "The Butterfly and the Moth", is by Tony Urquhart, and is reproduced by permission of the owner. The drawings for *The Dance of Death at London, Ontario* were prepared for the original edition by Jack Chambers, and are reproduced by permission of the artist. The drawings for *Twelve Letters to a Small Town* and *Two Chapters from an Emblem Book* are by James Reaney.

A Note on the Text

The poems in this collection are taken in part from printed versions, in part from the poet's own manuscripts and notebooks. Reaney's working methods are complicated; poems often take different forms over different periods, get published that way, and acquire an existence independent of later versions. "Yellow-Bellied Sapsucker," for example, is known in a later and quite independent form as "Gifts," which also appears as "the Existence poem" in *Colours in the Dark.* Similarly, "The Morning Dew" is an early version of "Alphabet." Not surprisingly, the manuscripts contain many half-finished poems in multiple versions, and there are aspects of Reaney's growth as a poet that cannot be represented here simply because the verse in which they are expressed has never taken publishable shape.

Nevertheless, a number of poems in this collection have not appeared before; these have been taken from manuscript, and their text has been approved by the poet. Others have already been printed elsewhere, and for them the poet prefers the printed to the manuscript version; they are reproduced here with only necessary corrections. A few previously published poems have not been reprinted; specialists can find them by using the bibliographies in the studies of Alvin Lee and Ross Woodman.

A few other points are worth noting: Certain early lyrics published before *The Red Heart* were heavily revised for that collection, and four of them are included here in both versions, because the differences between them were much commented on at the time. Poems that appear in *One-Man Masque* are given in their original versions here because Reaney does not wish to reject them (alternate forms can be found by consulting the text of *One-Man Masque* in *The Killdeer and Other Plays*). "The Dwarf," "The Baby," and "The Lost Child," which were part of a larger group of poems in *One-Man Masque*, are given here in an earlier arrangement, "A Sequence in Four Keys." As first planned, this sequence did not end with "The Lost Child" but with "The Hummingbird," and that poem can be found on another page. There are one or two eccentricities in the text arising from the practice of adhering closely to original printed versions; readers will notice the spelling of "gramaphone," which the poet seems to be fond of.

Wherever possible, the lines of the poems have been numbered in tens, though prose passages have made it difficult to do this everywhere.

1 POEMS 1945-49

Romanninth but Quakereleventh

Through the scribbler-paper clouds
The sun breaks with a scream
Like wrapping of a yellow crayon.
Elms that will be made into barns
With squeaking, tangling boughs
Sing like hoggstreet fiddlers.
Catfish and suckers and bream
Make a pewter-sparkle in the pond.
The muskrats in their lodges sleep
Like seeds in russet-apples.   10
Or as the smothered children do
Beneath the stairs in the old farm-house;
Where girls pluck a goose beside a fire
To stuff blue-striped feather-ticks,
Girls who have just learned to tell time
From a connecticut clock
Beside a fire that two years ago
Held orioles that sang door.
In the dark store-room
　　* * Christmas decorations * *   20
Reflect the dark store-room
The windows' staves are minuet
With white tea-leaves
And grey, gray wind.

1945

Play-box

If my step-father doesn't get much better
I don't suppose he will.
I will camp in a fence-corner
And be independent awhile.
The fence-corner where Effie
Lost her string of pearls
In an April-puddle
But in June we found them all again.
There I shall take my spotted ring
And the wool-blanket hemmed with red.   10
I shall set my clock up in a corner
Pears and grapes on its lid.
Also the corduroy suit
And the scarf with the purple bars
A pot of rouge in case I should ever go out.
The Illustrated News I'll get
And read it all the day
In June I'll eat wild strawberries
July there's a field of peaze.
In August the Duchess apples are ripe.   20

By that time I'll probably have
My play-box filled with old toys and scrap-books.
And poor dead butterfly wings.
No more hoeing for me
No more scrubbing of floors
No more holding of wood
While another chops dangerously near.
No more medicining horses
With their heads tied up to the roof
Nor any more calvings to watch   30
Kittens to drown or attempts to murther me.

4

When the ruts are white in Cardwell's Bush
As the Pork Street ballad goes
And the grain's all in that fall.
When the field-mice are all boarded
In the barn among the hay,
I shall take one walk across the fields.
Where the killdeers lie.
Lie buried and my father's horse in a corner
That we named after a judge.   40
And there are cow-horns sprinkled.

I shall shut myself up in my play-box hall.
Shut the lid; sleep the winter through.
With my toy green lantern for light.
They'll find me in the spring.

If I go to the orphanage
I will always dream of this . . .
My possible home in the fence-corner.
A spotted ring, a butterfly wing.
A green lantern's light.   50

1945

5

Maps

Five miles up from Pork Street
The maps hang on the wall
Gray-green windows on the world
Before which the scholars stand
And hear the gasp and roll atlantic
Above, like the cynosure of a Queen Anne's Lace Dance
The dark red island, Britain
Proud and proud.

O there are maps of Asia
Where warm winds blow   10
When outside the Janus-frost
Rules the bread-white snow.
A sultry Coil of breeze.
And a blossom.
Clogged winds of
Cinnamon and amber.

Fat yellow China
And purple India,
Ceylon like a chocolate comfit
The rim and dim ghost of Europe   20
Where the colour has run out . . .

Whenever we sing
"In days of yore"
We think of the New World's crown.
The green Northwest with its quaint inlets.
The brown Yukon.
Ungava bay and Newfoundland
Pink fevered Saskatchewan
And purple Alberta.

1945

The Antiquary

Within these jars and casks
I keep French and German moonlight
And that variety
That falls on the fieldish mouse
Crossing the floor of a farmer's kitchen.
I have chests of castles leprosied
By wind and by rain
Where young knights sigh
In iron purses.
Here are Wordsworth's vegetables   10
That teach a nobler life.
Here in these flasks
Lie the coughs of Emily Bronte,
The urine of Dr. John Donne,
And Jane Austen's caul.
Here is Queen Anne's seventh child
Pickled in liquor . . .

1946

Night Train

Night:
A Guyfawkes hesitation.
Shallwillshall it go.
The wheels have chilblains.
Will the trees let the train pass?
Will the pond reflect the yellow light?
There is a dead caterpillar of smoke
Horizontal and stalagmite
And the first bar of annielaurie
In a minor-key at Sebben's crossing.   10
All the way from Stratford to Shakespeare
The night-train trails a stream
Of light brown hair
Until the curls come out finally
Into a fine tea-colored mist.
Each night she moans by
With her wig of nut-brown curls.

1946

Decadence

O Lord
These days
These fallen into evil
Fallen into weevil
Days,
When gipsies ride in cars
And farmers wear underwear
And people do not know
Who or what sliced their bread.

1946

The Hollyhocks (1936)

In June and May
There are many green mountains.
In the garden
Beneath the windowsill
And along the edges of fields
Where farmers shout gee and haw.

Perhaps to commemorate Confederation
A white gander steps out at the bottom
Of each green hill
And climbs slowly to the summit.   10
Where he disappears into air
That is surely on a diet
Or fasting the saints.

1946

9

Faces and the Drama in a Cup of Tea

The cup had the outlines of a cup
In a lantern-slide.
And it was filled with Congou tea
What did it mean this cup of tea?
Perhaps the law of eight times seven
Will change some day.
Some teacher's cheek
Will blush in realized mistake.
It will be a sort of city-sunset on her cheek
Reflected in the window of a seamstress.   10
She will say:
The whole universe lies on a window-sill,
A speck of sulphur or a slowly dying pin,
Bloodying in rust.
A speck of sulphur on a shelf
A dying pin turning to bloodred rust.
Then there will come a strange deny of time.
Various street-cries embroidered in the mist.

1946

Kodak (1927)

Miss ffrench and Brownshoes
(For many years we gave Brownshoes
Large benefits of doubt).
Have come to see my garden.
Noiselessly, they walk
The winding worms of air
That are its paths.
They pat the childish sunflowers
Regard the fragments of Mary's Dress
The Forget-me-nots display,   10
And swoom low over the moss-roses.
Miss ffrench is dressed in the fashion of the year.
A narrow egyptian frock.
Brownshoes' moustache is like
Two gold-fish, leaping for his nose.
Officiously, like a little widow, the orchard-grass
Has wept its dew upon their shoes.
The gold thread that hems Miss ffrench's dress
Seems to say in Morse, ahem.
Her shoes are moving up and down   20
As breasts with breath.
They have their camera.
No one sits in its gloomy parlour
Of pleated walls.
No wind stirs or ghost stalks,
Except the very large eye of God.
Miss ffrench makes God wink
("You'd better let me take it this time
You're too nervous")
And all my garden . . .   30
And all my garden stands suddenly imprisoned
Within her pleated den.

1946

These Wicked Streets

Where would I simple weeds
On these wicked streets.
The tinkle of a chamber-pot
Falling from bed-room windows
Of a blind-drawn lonely
House of bawds.
These gray streets
Lit with tungsten wicks in leaking cups
Of yellow.
These streets, wicked sentences   10
From necromancer's books
Streets enclosing cellars,
Brontean potatoes
And lidding rivers, creeks and streams.

1946

Childhood Musette

So long ago
The dry snow
Whirled up at me
In a cloud of whey
As I walked down
With my mother a pillar
Of dark fur behind me
Down Wellington Street
That in summer is gray
As a straight stream of sleet   10
And in winter is white
As a splinter of light.
Down Wellington street went we
By the public and pubic dark
Cubic and conic large
Christmas Tree.

So long ago
The purple sloe
From beneath the eaves
Of its green leaves   20
Looked out at me with a wicked grin
"For they use us you know to flavour gin."
While all around me the sun did shine
In yellow spokes of yellow wine.

So far away these things
As if they are fragile rings so thin
I hardly dare wear them.
As far away they seem to cry
As very white stars set up in the sky
Like white notes pricked for such a lute   30
As must make all other music mute.

1947

13

Madame Moth

Madame Moth
Like a little brown tract
Like a pamphlet of four pages
Flaps through the blackness of the night
To my candle that so enrages
Her love of soft and wicked darkness
For straight stands its golden spire
A spear of innocent noise.
And she flops about
Around and around its yellow cry   10
And I could have caught her
Had not she
Hugged my candle out
With her brown sloppy wings.
Then I couldn't see anywhere
And now her dark mouth sings
And she crawls all over my face and hands
"You must do now my dark demands."

1947

Mrs. Wentworth

I was tired of evenings of euchre
Of waltzing and dancing with fools.
There was nothing to look at in the sky.
The moon had disappeared
And the stars bore me.

Ink gleams wet only a moment
After a person writes.
So I gleamed only a moment
After eighteen years with a Wentworth.
Now Mr. Wentworth was a prominent practitioner   10
Of one of the religions of this city.

I was sick of reading Spurgeon
I was tired of singing Moody
I was positive I wouldn't burgeon
In the Congregational Choir.
And I thought I once had been saved
Ship Ahoy
And I once had been laved
In the precious blood of the Lamb
Ship Ahoy and Rescue the perishing.   20
It was then I decided
That I
Would have looked rather silly
On a cross.

Then I took to taking walks in the country
Just at the edge of town
(The houses like runs in rummy.)
With a certain Mr. O'Flaherty.
We smelt the fields of buckwheat together.
In those days I had a lump   30
On the white back of my neck
And he sang to me

That when I would kiss him real hard
He'd give me a handkerchief
For my inside coat-pocket
And a handkerchief for my outside coat-pocket
And he said he knew some liniment
To take my lump away.

But he gave me a swelling in front
And now I fear the Lord.   40
Oh give me a grenade against him
I cannot stand his toasted smile
And his red hair.
And oh what shall I do
When the roll is called up yonder?
There is nothing to look at in the sky
The moon has disappeared
And the stars bore me.

1947

The Gramaphone

Upon the lake
At Gramaphone
A beastly bird
Sits on the bank
And dips its beak
Of sharpened bone
Into a haunted
Tank
That ripples with an eternal stone.

When the ladies descend the stairs,   10
Some eat their fans
And others comb their hair.
But Miss Mumblecrust
Picks up that beastly bird
And dips its beak
Into that round lake
That ripples with eternal stone
And dips its beak of sharpened bone
Into a pool of a young man singing
"I'm all alone   20
By the telephone!"

1947

17

!! Warning !!

THE TRAPPING SEASON
FOR ALL SORTS OF FUR
HAS OPENED ON THE AVENUE ST. CLAIR
Through the wind's shriek
(Like a tortured Bolshevik)
The women slink by
In skunk and raccoon
Wombat's fur and Duck-billed
Platypus catsfur and dogsfur
Lynx muffs and bearskins   10
The pelts of weasels and jackasses
Wolfskins and rabbitskins
Ratskins and mouseskin
Sheepskin and cowhide
Horsehide and apeskin
For their hearts
Sink in fear
Since it is the trapping season
On the Avenue St. Clair.

Even old Mr. Bluett   20
Is afraid
He may be shot
For his dragoon moustache.
It would make such a
Suitable
Wrap.
The traps are baited
With pieces of cake
Irresistible and chocolate eclairs.
Hear the ladies scream   30
On the Avenue St. Clair
As fastidious jaws
Bite into limb or paw.
Hear the mysterious trappers rush forth
(In the wind-shriek)
To see how much their prey is worth.
(Like a tortured Bolshevik.)

1947

18

The Stove Pipe

WHATWHAT is this?
There must be a lady in the house.
She's a blackamoor.

Down through the kitchen-ceiling
A fat, swollen round leg
Washes its foot in the stove.

If I take up the stove-lids
I will see her feet . . .
If I run upstairs
I may see her face.   10

No lady here.
For here her legs continue
Into the chimneys.
She is probably
Sitting on the roof.

1947

A Prayer

Water obeys the rules set down
Of creeks and rivers, oceans and fountains
Of china and glass and crockery
But I, O Lord, only Thy Dish
In which you apparently placed me;
A Dish of Desires. Which are
Gold wallpaper, cake and tea
Someone playing or singing
An Oboe
Or a Banjo   10
A white-toothed piano.
Die for me if you must, dear God
But please keep these things overflowing.

1947

Tarzan jad guru

Young muscular Edwardian
  Swings through trees,
  Stops carnage at Karnak,
  Whole trains at Windhoek,
  Dances waltzes simianese.
Lord Greystoke jad guru.

A dumb yellow drum
  Hangs down from the night.
  For the rite of the Dum Dum
  Come the cousin apes.   *10*
  He who could wear Bond Street
  And opera capes
  Prefers loin cloths of
  Impeccable cut.
Lady Jane Greystoke jad guru.

Mazumba waves his spear!
  Oh the white beach and the green palms!
  Stygian night between the ears!
  Oh Prince of slaughter do not bungle
  My jugular vein within the jungle,   *20*
  And springboks flee across the plains
  From apes with silver headed canes.
Edward VII jad guru!

1947

* The seventh of the Tarzan books has a language Edgar
Rice Burroughs invented for the prehistoric people
Tarzan meets on the other side of a mysterious African
lake: "jad guru" means the "Terrible". Also, Tarzan's
real name is Lord Greystoke.

           34725

Tillie the Toiler

Music of transcribed financial guano
Miss Toiler plays upon her strange piano
  Margot travaille bien

Like a galloping pale kaiserina
And a leafy filing tsarina
  Margot travaille bien

The rain upon the window strums
On churches and gymnasiums
  Margot travaille bien

The salesman's aching thighs await   10
Masonic Hall for dancing date
  Margot travaille bien

Afterwards in the car he took it out
The rain upon the roof
Was her ten fingers typing stout
  Margot travaille bien

1947

The Birth of Venus

I
In and underneath
The warm sea breathing
Up and down
Feverish-breasted with waves
White legs of papier-mache assemble.
A torso of pink rubber
Has holes for long wooden arms
A wool and marble head
And room for the giant lover
Expectant upon the peacock-spotted marble shore.   10

II
Apples fall like desultory tennis
In the dark orchard where chaste stout trees
Stiffly fondle fondly
Whose roots flow like purple brooks
Over the ground-hog hollow earth.
We lie so close
Upon the grass
The gunpowder in our thick-twigged hearts
Dreams of the fiercest command
So that our two hearts rush out   20
Like two red star-shells bursting from
The toothless mouths of cannon
Killing each other instantly
Among the demisemiquaver cricket cries
In the hush between the falls of pears
Like moons and stars in a green sky
Appear upon the green-needled lawn.
And sad old trees with bellies
Watch us
Until there is only one shadow between us   30
Until we have swallowed each other's
Fish-eyed soul
Until the red hair and branches
That lace and lightning the night
Of our limbs
Enmeshes entangles
Inextricably
In one explosive
Fated glow
While we lie in each other   40
Like one river
Drowning face down
In another river.

III
In the brown darkness
Of the earth beneath us
Lies the dead groundhog
Who died in bed.
Here in the starless fog
The subterranean branches
Of the ancient orchard   50
Wage battle
For night-soil and corpses.
These skull-sized apples
Mean the late-discovered shroud
Of the murthered child
Transformed into a hundred
Red gouts and gobbets
Of yellow wood and red blood.
So beneath our counterpane
Country of march-pane joy   60
Lie hate and death, battle
And conflicting rusty saws and
Orange-speckled swords.
From this love
This death of death
Up seventy gray stairs
Runs the eager messenger
To hang out
The very red eye of death again itself.

1947

FIRST PUBLISHED VERSIONS OF FOUR "RED HEART" POEMS

i) The School Globe

He dreamt he held the world,
(A slippery skull within his arms)
And would not let it go,
This glazed reticule filled with
Gold, lead and fire for volcanoes.

He woke to find it was
A broken globe, a cracked sphere
Filled with dying apricots
And decadent pears, melons
And other broken fruit.   10
All these were the toys and pets
Of a childhood and a youth
A house where he was little
And afraid to swear
Because the Lord might hear
And send a bear;
Of places where he had been young ⌐
Sniffed the pink clenches,
The white and pink fists
Of roses; watched the rain   20
That heaven's clouds threw down
In splinters and sheets
Of soft brown glass upon the ground.

This was the parcel of his past,
This was the basket of pluperfect,
A broken globe, a hollow sphere
Filled with torn orchardry.

1946

ii) The Death of the Poet *

Above me the sun is hanging
From a tree.
Heavy the sun
Dragging down the branch.
My heart hangs heavy
The only leaf
Upon a red tree.
Heavy the heart that
Will not fall loose when
Autumn comes   10
But bring tree, bough and branch
To a gray bed.

When the stars stare
With yellow eyes
From their dark high chairs
Placed at the top
Of a black stairs
When the night is
Brown and black
Like Congou tea   20
Then the sunflowers
And other flowers
Touch the ground
And strive to see
Through the earth
To the sun.

When they open my grave
To steal my watch and ring
I'll not be there
But gone burrowing   30
For the sun
That hangs heavy
Dragging down the protesting branch
Bough and branch.
The sun that is my heart
The only leaf
Upon a red tree
Heavyheavyheavyheavy
To a gray grave.

1946

* The Red Heart

26

iii) The Heart and the Sun

Come to me, cried the Heart to the Star.
The Heart like a red lute
Thus sang to its gold lover;
Stand in me and kindle
My breathing beating,
Those soft footsteps
That in my streets
March on an eternity.

Come to me, cried the Heart to the Star.
The Heart like a red bell   10
Dangled in a crooked steeple
Thus sang to its gold beloved.
Ring me and kindle
My breathing beating.
Toll out my peculiar voice
The peal that sings on an eternity.

Into the Heart's red cage
Then ran the young Sun.
Into the dungeon
Where like the prisoner of a Maze   20
His footsteps did ticktock
25000 days,
I have caught you, cried the Heart
In Love to the trapped yellow Wanderer.

When the winter-time comes
The Heart like a fat lilac leaf
Swings ripely heavy
On the branch of its red tree
And drops to a gray grave.
Then the gold prisoner wears away   30
And rusts out his russet case,
Flies out the burst heart
Crying, as he looks at his dead red mistress
And her sweet dungeons and rooms
That now swarm with decay,
Alas, it is my fate
To smother what I kindle
To engender what I'll kill.

1946

27

iv) Antichrist as a Child

Like the yellow willow-leaf
Of a lighted candle
I crookedly waver
Here in my mother's garden,
Why does she look sadly
Out of an upstairs window at me?
Why does she stare so
At the pale straw star of me
As I wander in my soot-coloured cloak
Down and through this garden?   10
Why do the flowers avoid my fingers
And turn away their pink stars
Pale as windows recollected in the mind?
Why do my shoes hurt
Until they bleed but still
I must not let on to anyone
About the hooves.
I must wear shoes
Or they will shoot me for a monster.

Am I so monstrous?   20

Why do I dream of eclipses
Of ruined cities beneath zeppelins in sunsets
And inverted churches?

1946

The Dead Rainbow

I
As she walks down the tapeworm street
How like a heart her footsteps beat
As if each paver bleated
Of a life beneath it heated,
Within a cellared, withered swoon,
By a mildewed, buried moon
That lies in the world's hull
Like a white puffball skull.
With myrrh her clock-like heart is fed

As she hurried to her lover's bed.   *10*
Her heart-like footsteps speak of a soldier
Soldered to her shoulder.
The footsteps in her clock-heart scurry
To a fair thin man named Alfred Murray.
Like two gates they shall close together
And loose another heart from its tether
Hidden in a town besieged by cranes
Huddled in Mr Murray's reins.

When her heart and his heart
With mad red whey smart   *20*
Like two red clouds over
This city they hover
Until they attain
A strepitoso rain
That raises the dust in these streets in a wave
From out of its flat thin sinless grave,
That chases the dwarves from chaos through mazes
To be caesars, kaisers, mutes and jackasses,
For the clock-like rain of their hearts to the gate
Is a summons for which none may hesitate   *30*
In that secret town besieged by cranes
In Mister Alfred Murray's reins.

These gates in their shutting
Imply a whimper's butting
As the once-closed gate is burst
And forth to the funeral hearse
From a scrotal city innocent
A screeching pigmy's sent
Sent to grow larger but finally bent
Back to the fine dust's yellow Lent   *40*
For the wicked endless windlass from a Well
Lifts one only down another shaft of Hell.

II
Slow against the dead rainbow
Of the vertebrate street
That flows past my window
Her sullen feet grate
As if Death knocked a rusty nail
Into her coffin
Through her heart
That's soft as a muffin.   50
In her room she will die
On her hard bed
Lit by a square sigh
Of dead sky.
She will perish unwed
Unringed and unravished.
And outside the winds neigh
To rush her dust away
In a shape like an eel
Or a rotting automobile   60
And let her down
Into that scrotal town
Ever threatened by red crowds
Of heart-shaped clouds
That in the myrrh-breathed weather
Entwine fast together
And let down vines to raise
From the dust
The roars and brays
Of asses and lions   70
That hide
In that unremembered weather of the loins.
There she will lie until
Two hearts will
Beat upon the window-pane
Of her dust-drenched brain
The breath and infection
Of Lust's resurrection
That but ends in the graveyard's harvest
Of stooks and sheaves of stone   80
Buoys to mark the place where rest
In a wooden submarine
Sunk in the grave's latrine
White dead sailors sparsely carved from bone.

III
Oh the poor little sad little laundress
Is a very mad maid and wanderess
On the bright white tail of the centauress
That is the mode road and egress
From the streets sad as a negress
Of this old world whirled a mote   *90*
In the eye of a star-moated remote
God God God God God God
And as she races
Down the mazes
Of the centauresses' tail
That winds in the grass like a creek
Of water creaking pale
From a sea in the moon,
Through the gold afternoon
Plantagenet men roam home   *100*
From a study of the women in Rome
And in supposition most antic
Wind up the gigantic
Sharpest old pyramid
With a gryphon's glass eye-lid
For lewd and deluded
Their brains love-diluted
They suppose it a stone metronome.
SHE wanders sad past
Woods filled with mast   *110*
And cake-pillared pavilions
Where in love-drowsy millions
Lovers and loveresses glide
And softly collide;
In dresses of silver, men and women
Dressed in moans of moon-linen
White as a negress albino
Dancing in a pitchblende casino,
By once rugged seas now drugged
With a horde of drowned demirugs   *120*
Pushed from the sills
Of Scotland filled with skulls
By the death of great Macbeth
But from the sack
Of each track
That her feet

Print in the street
Filled with the white hail
Of the centauress' tail
Springs another wild laundress,   130
For each step of the wanderess
In the snow of the centaur-hair
Is a love-affair
Of forgetfulness
And breeds only more loud breathing
And more bread for Death.

IV
Through the streets
Wandering sweetly
Like the sound of a bell
From Heaven's steeples   140
Even as it must sound
To those of Hell's peoples
That live in the sore of sin
And are fed on molten tin
Soundlessly there flows an angel
Like a girl composed of rose-coloured noise
Like a boy in paduasoy leading two talbothoys
But without a heart or footstep
For the ticking I hear
Is not of pulse, blood or foot   150
Beating the white street
But the sound of his watch
Ringing with the World's centuries
Raging with every hour and every life
And the hands of that clock
Are clogged feet that walk
And flow ever more slowly
For this angel has decreed
With a bribe of blood
The cessation of erection   160
From the yellow streets of dust
In the scrotal town of lust.
He has refused to wind
Up the neighing death-wind
That sweeps the dead into living.

Birth and decay
This bell-like angel
Shall lay away.
He shall end the mad jig
In a tumbril whirligig   170
Whose occupant wears a wig
Of panting lecherous leeches
That penetrate the brain
In the rain of footsteps
Down the vertebrate
Street to the hard bed where grate
The gates that do not shed misery
Or shut out grief disease and pain
But only upon future windowpanes
Drum the rain of more.   180
Of more
Instead of
Nevermore.
Instead of down with the sound
And the notion and the mention
Of sands whirring in hourglasses
Of endless impregnable windlasses
And pregnant glass ladies
Swollen up by ravishing glassblowers
Of the codlike pendulum   190
And the heart-like drum,
For in pity this angel
Has dipped and washed
The watch of us in his blood
Abolished Hell
And cooled Desire
With the cold fire of his blood
So that as he walks through the town
Our clock-like hearts run ever down.
O MERCIFUL ANGEL   200
WHO HAS DELIVERED US FROM HELL.

1948

33

Platonic Love

My love, I've watched you
All this summer afternoon I've watched you
Lying in the field in the sun
A pink heap of cloth and flesh in the grass
Your hat beside you was half full of berries
Which you must have picked where I am standing.
Then you turned lazy and lay down
In the summer sun and I came
Through the dark thick woods
To the edge of your field where I leaned   10
Against this fence post in the brambles.
The shadows of the trees flowed down to you
But I couldn't, although my shadow did.
It almost touched you before you left,
Almost, — until you looked up and saw
The black tide of shade coming at you
And walked home through brighter fields.

I did not dare come down to you because
I loved you, the shoddiest reason of all.
But now that you have gone, of course,   20
I run down the field to where you lay.
I stand and lie beside and walk around
The grass where you have slept.
That grass is all bent where you were, you know
And different. It will still be different
Months from now and makes a green lady,
A green gingerbread man of pressed down grass;
A flat green girl of bent shiny hay
Is all that lies where you have been.
What were you thinking of?   30
Oh God, this is all I'll have of you,
This is the nearest we shall be
As I lie beside this green thin phantom.
This green ghost where you have lain
Shall whirl with me down
And down, until I die,
Down and down the wells and passageways of Time.
Light as newspaper floating on the streets
This my green hollow love.

Come sit on my knee, green emptiness   40
Here's a kiss for you, puff-of-air.
Come into my bed, green miss,
Green marionette, and I will be
Monsieur Ventriloquist
Forcing you to say you love me
And all too easily making you say it.
What light green arms you have, my dear.
What lovely light and green limbs
And your face! And your green flowing hair!
If I leave you here in this field   50
I know where to find you
Even when you've faded away in the rain
And are covered with snow, even
Next year I shall be able to dig you up,
Green Girl.
But God I am sick of watching where Love lies
And sick of shadow girls
Kissing shadow guys.

1949

Winter's Tales

As planets love an ancient star
And move in far dances round its fire
So the farmer and his children sit
About their stove whose flamey wit
Giggles in red and yellow laughter
Like a small sun caught in iron armour.
When outside the winter winds are loud
Close by their summery stove they crowd.

Through the windows they may see
The cold wind herd a river of snow   10
Beneath the moon, across the land
All locked in Winter's frog-cold hand.
And sometimes the wind does shove
Between the window sill and window
Beneath the door and across the floor
White whisks and brooms of snow.
Through every little crack
At the front door and the back
Came the soft white hands of snow
That, with its heat, the stove does smash   20
Into a harmless flat thin splash.
Then down the chimney the wind came
Till the fire seemed somewhat lame
Until someone poked at it
Or put on another stick
And it blazed up again.
The wind, the cold snow and the rain
Could not put that stove out
But in a furious dance
They kept a safe distance   30
Always beyond the window pane
So that the farmer and his children
By the stove sitting tight
Only heard the wind and never felt
Its sharp cold bite.
Then the farmer told them stories
That his father had told him
Of the massacre at Lucan
Where the neighbors killed all of the McKilligans dead
Except one little boy who crawled under a bed;   40
Of the little boy carried off by a bear
And, "a ball of fire leaped out of the earth
At him and vanished into thin air.

Your grandmother saw
Tecumseh's head on a pole;
Had also dined with him once
And when she looked into her soup
At the bottom of the bowl
She saw a groundhog's paw.
And Indian Sal who picked flax   50
And drank vinegar and had attacks
And Granny Crack
Who wandered the countryside
With seven petticoats to her back.
And Towser Smith who
When it rained for five days in a row
Went out and shook his fist at the sky,
His fist at God in the sky.
And how when I was a child
You stood at the table   60
And ate off a pie-tin
Not sit on chairs and eat off a plate
As you do now.
And how bricks and mortar
Couldn't keep her from marrying him."
Then the farmer and his children grow drowsy
With the heat of the fire so blowsy
And the stories their father tells them
Of the good and bad old days
Grow shorter and shorter   70
Till the fire alone seems to talk.
Its ripening red now seeming
A massive convulsive giant's heart
A Robin's red breast.
A sunset in summer,
The rising and large Harvest Moon
When she walks out of the east, —
All these things seems the fire
Which, with their father's stories
Will long be remembered   80
And protect them from growing old.
Winter's tales that like gold
In the purses of their hearts
Will ring and shine forever
Warming them in the long winter's cold.

1949

37

The Canadian

How sad it is, this winter farmhouse parlour
Coloured like the bindings of religious books,
Dull green, brown and dingy maroon,
And the stove as black as a bible.
And Grandfather in his picture looks
Reproachful, as if to say
You can't sit here reading!
Isn't there anything you can do?
Did I clear this farm for this?
To which I reply: It's Sunday   10
And I'll loll in idleness here
As long as I want to, Grandpa Dear,
With occasional glances at a treatise on law;
(Your terrific success at chopping up wood, Grandpa,
Has enabled your son to go to Osgoode.)
Besides which I'm reading Foxe's *Martyrs*,
How they put Saint Jude in a hollow log
And sawed that log in seven pieces.
There's a very good illustration   20
In which they're making a seventh saw.
I yawn and look at the clock
Or the picture of a collie-dog
Lying on his master's grave
At which I've often cried,
Or the print of the Fathers of Confederation
Or a view of the Windmills at Boom
Things that pass for decoration
In this dowdy stuffy room
Where I sit in the centre of the Christmas vacation   30
Alone, with only the ticking clock
For Company, and the fire and the wind outside.

The frost upon the windowpanes
Seems South Sea Islands there
Whose still and stiff white palms of ice
No South Wind rearranges
With warm soft arms of air.
This stove I'm sitting by
With the heat of its orange fire
Makes this room seem shifted   40
Out of this wintry season
To a stifled hot July.
I get up and hands in pockets
Look through the icy window
Upon the sea of snow

Whose white and chilly waves
Have drowned all summer's sailors
The green leaves and the oriole's song
The bee-speckled winds
The black moth in the long grass,   50
All these lie in their graves
With the long shadows of an eight o'clock sunset
With the vanished jewels of summer dew
All somewhere beneath this wig of snow
Where in the gray sky the feeble sun
Low in the sky to the south is hung
And where, bottled up in this warm windless dungeon,
I watch from this parlour window.

I long for hot lands
Where cocoa trees grow   60
That bend in the trade wind breeze
That has flowed through gay bands
Of precious spice plants
And orange and lemon trees
Where birds fly who never leave
Sadly for the South
Where flowers grow that never grieve
With terror of the frost
And there are palms
Beneath whose green spokes   70
Chant and dance the heathen folks
Who have no laws
And whose clothes
Are the blessed winds that surround them
And perhaps a feather
And whose consciences
So fattened in us by this weather
Have never found them.

So I long in this dark parlour,
Dull green, brown and maroon,   80
The colour of starling feathers,
This stuffy dingy room.
These dreams of tropical weathers!
My grim grandfather!
The Fathers of Confederation!
These windows embossed
With a mocking white imitation
Of what I wish for, in frost.

1949

39

2 THE RED HEART-1949

I THE PLUM TREE

The Plum Tree

The plums are like blue pendulums
That thrum the gold-wired winds of summer.
In the opium-still noon they hang or fall,
The plump, ripe plums.
I suppose my little sister died
Dreaming of looking up at them,
Of lying beneath that crooked plum tree,
That green heaven with blue stars pied.
In this lonely haunted farmhouse
All things are voiceless save the sound   10
Of some plums falling through the summer air
Straight to the ground.
And there is no listener, no hearer
For the small thunders of their falling
(Falling as dead stars rush to a winter sea)
Save a child who, lolling
Among the trunks and old featherticks
That fill the room where he was born,
Hears them in his silent dreaming
On a dark engraving to a fairy-tale forlorn.   20
Only he hears their intermittent soft tattoo
Upon the dry, brown summer ground
At the edge of the old orchard.
Only he hears, and farther away,
Some happy animal's slow, listless moo.

The Clouds

Whitely the clouds come
Across this afternoon
While I sit, as at play,
And watch where far away
The clouds weep
And shake with thunderous laughter.
But, nearer, glide
In continual melancholy
Neither with sadness nor gladness
Like a dream of sheep.   10

Then all I know is that it's sometime
In the humdrum green summertime
And all the sky's become
A bedroom's wallpaper
Where vague white beasts
Jostle, slip and caper.
There are white fat sheep
After whom the winds leap
And white jumping mountains
Whose feet are downward fountains   20
And who creak and creep and fly
Down the bright summer sky.
All walk on long tall stilts of glass
For too close they dare not pass
For fear for gold
They might be caught and sold.
There are hundreds of pairs
Of pink sofas and chairs
And great pink lutes
And soft pink boots   30
Pink swollen violins

Fat naked gentlemen whose sins
Have made them fat
And at least a vat
Of swans and gramaphones.
Then I woke and they were clouds again
Composed of swiftly sculptured rain.
They were only clouds
And not the fascinating crowds
Of fat furniture that capered   40
On those blue walls wallpapered
By the Marchioness of Madness.
Still,
What are the clouds that sail by so slow
In pale cities of wrestling snow
If not that fancied wallpaper where rang
The soft marvellous bells of delirious meringue?

The Sundogs

I saw the sundogs barking
On either side of the Sun
As he was making his usual will
And last testament
In a glorious vestment.
And the sundogs cried,
"Bow wow!
We'll make a ring
Around the moon
And children, seeing it, will say: 10
Up there they play Farmer in the Dell
And the moon like the cheese stands still.
Bow wow!
We shall drown the crickets,
Set the killdeer birds crying,
Send shingles flying,
And pick all the apples
Ripe or not.
Our barking shall overturn
Hencoops and rabbit-hutches,   20
Shall topple over privies
With people inside them,
And burn with invisible,
Oh, very invisible!
Flames
In each frightened tree.
Whole branches we'll bite off
And for the housewife's sloth
In not taking them in
We'll drag her sheets and pillow cases   30
Off the fence
And dress up in them

And wear them thin.
And people will say
Both in the country
And in the town
It falls in pails
Of iron nails.
We'll blow the curses
Right back into the farmer's mouths   40
As they curse our industry
And shake their fists,
For we will press the oats
Close to the ground,
Lodge the barley,
And rip open the wheat stooks.
We shall make great faces
Of dampness appear on ceilings
And blow down chimneys
Till the fire's lame.   50
With the noise of a thousand typewriters
We shall gallop over the roofs of town.
We are the Sun's animals.
We stand by him in the West
And ready to obey
His most auburn wish
For Rain, Wind and Storm."

Suns and Planets

Suns and planets of the sky
When will you be ripe and die?
Will a great wind sometime sweep
The dark branches where you weep
And dash and pluck and throw
Venus and Mars and gray Pluto
Like pears, apples and plums upon the ground
(Red, yellow and gold, oval and round)
To grow mildewed and ragged there
Softening the thick autumn air   10
With your piebald rays' decay?

The Crow

A fool once caught a crow
That flew too near even for his stone's throw.
Alone beneath a tree
He examined the black flier
And found upon its sides
Two little black doors.
He opened both of them.
He expected to see into
Perhaps a little kitchen
With a stove, a chair,   10
A table and a dish
Upon that table.
But he only learned that crows
Know a better use for doors than to close
And open, and close and open
Into dreary, dull rooms.

Whither do you Wander?

Whither do I wander
Beneath the sun and moon?
Often into some dead garden
Whose stiff dead leaves
Are languageless with frost,
All forsaken, all forlorn
Where waits an old woman
Who, with a beckon, offers gold
For one's tonsils and one's fingers
With which, she says, she mends   10
Her rakes and curry-combs
With which she combs and strokes
The massy fur and manes
Of her two great black hounds
And of her great black horse.
Next I may come
To a sly fox's den.
He is as charming and good-mannered
As the President of France,
But his kitchen-floor he's scrubbing   20
With a tub of blood.
So that wherever I go,
Wherever I wander
I never find
What I should like to find;
For example, a mother and father
Who loved me dearly
And loved each other so,
And brothers and sisters with whom,
In the summer, I'd play hide-and-go-seek 30
And in the winter, in the snow,
Fox-and-goose week after week.
Instead I must forever run
Down lanes of leafless trees
Beneath a Chinese-faced sun;
Must forsaken and forlorn go
Unwanted and stepmotherishly haunted
Beneath the moon as white as snow.

49

The Heart and the Sun

"Come to me!" cried the Heart to the Star.
The Heart like a lute, like a red guitar
Thus sang out to its golden lover.
"Stand here within me and kindle
My beating, pulsive breathing;
Pray start those soft footsteps
That in my streets
May march a century."

"Come to me!" gasped the Heart to the Star.
The Heart like a red bell   10
Hanging in a walking steeple
Thus sang to its gold beloved.
"Ring me, begin my beating
So that my new, peculiar voice
May sing at last."

Into the Heart's red cage
Then ran the young Sun.
Into its blood-filled dungeon
Where like the prisoner of a Maze
His footsteps of Sunsets and Sunrises   20
Did ticktock five times 5,000 days.
"You are mine! I have caught you!"
Cried the Heart
In her love for the trapped yellow wanderer.

Then came, long after, the winter
When ripely heavy with age
The Heart like a red leaf
Fell from her branch
Into a grave and gray grave.
Pulled by the fierce winter wind   30
Plucked down by the bold winter cold
The Heart fell from life
And the gold prisoner within her
With swift rust
Wore away her red, russet walls.
When out of that broken heart he flew
He wept and did sadly survey
His dead red mistress
Whose sweet rooms and dungeons
Now swarmed and whirred with decay.   40
"Alas, my Love, it is your fate and mine
That I someday smother whom I kindle
And give birth to those I'll someday kill."

50

The Red Heart

The only leaf upon its tree of blood,
My red heart hangs heavily
And will never fall loose,
But grow so heavy
After only a certain number of seasons
(Sixty winters, and fifty-nine falls,
Fifty-eight summers, and fifty-seven springs)
That it will bring bough
Tree and the fences of my bones
Down to a grave in the forest   10
Of my still upright fellows.

So does the sun hang now
From a branch of Time
In this wild fall sunset.
Who shall pick the sun
From the tree of Eternity?
Who shall thresh the ripe sun?
What midwife shall deliver
The Sun's great heir?
It seems that no one can,   20
And so the sun shall drag
Gods, goddesses and parliament buildings,
Time, Fate, gramaphones and Man
To a gray grave
Where all shall be trampled
Beneath the dancing feet of crowds
Of other still-living suns and stars.

Clouds

These clouds are soft fat horses
That draw Weather in his wagon
Who bears in his old hands
Streaked whips and strokes of lightning.
The hooves of his cattle are made
Of limp water, that stamp
Upon the roof during a storm
And fall from dripping eaves;
Yet these hooves have worn away mountains
In their trotting over Earth.   10
And for manes these clouds
Have the soft and various winds
That still can push
A ship into the sea
And for neighs, the sable thunder.

The Royal Visit

When the King and the Queen came to Stratford
Everyone felt at once
How heavy the Crown must be.
The Mayor shook hands with their Majesties
And everyone presentable was presented
And those who weren't have resented
It, and will
To their dying day.
Everyone had almost a religious experience
When the King and Queen came to visit us   10
(I wonder what they felt!)
And hydrants flowed water in the gutters
All day.
People put quarters on the railroad tracks
So as to get squashed by the Royal Train
And some people up the line at Shakespeare
Stayed in Shakespeare, just in case—
They did stop too,
While thousands in Stratford
Didn't even see them   20
Because the Engineer didn't slow down
Enough in time.
And although,
But although we didn't see them in any way
(I didn't even catch the glimpse
The teacher who was taller did
Of a gracious pink figure)
I'll remember it to my dying day.

Pink and White Hollyhocks

In June and July
Green spires
Spear in my garden
Beneath the windowsills
And along the edges of those fields
Where the farmers shout gee and haw
And in the ditches
Where girls picking strawberries
Say tee and hee.

Within those green towers   10
Ladies pre-raphaelite
In their intense ascent
Climb slowly to the topmost rooms
With pink lamps and white lanterns.
Never do they pause
For the windows gleam pink and white
From July to September.

When in autumn
The garden is dying,
They enter the highest chamber,   20
Hung with citherns and lutes,
Lie down with their lover,
Blow out the pink lamps forever.

Gray Pillar

Alone in the farmhouse am I.
Cyclopean eye in the thisway
And the thatway of bannisters
And staircases; mouseholes
Like the eyes of skeletons
And wardrobes and closets
Whose intestines are old dresses.
Beneath and downstairs
With ice-tones
The clock strikes.   *10*

I see a little pond
Exquisite upon a Christmas card
Filled with one excited skater.
He strikes with delicate foot
Twelve times
The bell-like ice of clean water
Turned to glass.
Never never shall the ice melt
Nor the excited skater cease
To write upon glass with diamond foot   *20*
My life and love and childhood,
Although the yellow old willow nearby
Surrounded by this modern floor of ice
Reminds us of our deathfullness;
This yellowness, these gold veins and aiteries
Flowing, flowering into a wintry sky
That has a gray breast-bone
Speak all as mortal . . .
Still, these things shall never die.
The blue wind that blew   *30*
The scraping skater
And the mohock star
That scraped upon my window-pane pond
The names of my german,
The names of my leman,
The hour of my birthday,
The maze and passageways,
The rage and laziness
Of all my life.

The Upper Canadian

I wish I had been born beside a river
Instead of this round pond
Where the geese white as pillows float
In continual circles
And never get out.

Sometimes I wish that I
Hadn't been born in this dull township
Where fashion, thought and wit
Never penetrate,
Unless the odd quotation from *Handy Andy*   10
Is really what I demand,
What I want.

The river, the railroad,
And His Majesty's Highways
Number Seven and Eight
Go through town
And never are the same again.
But this pond and I
Go through and become
Nothing different.   20
Now if I went away
And left this little lake,
If I struck out for the railroad and the river,
I might lose my way.
I would have to win a scholarship
Or build a Punch and Judy Show.
I'd better not,
I'd better stay.

And watch the darning-needle flies
Fly and glitter in the shining wind   *30*
Of summer by this pond.
At night I'll read
The Collected Works of William Shakespeare
By an empty stove
And think at least there's this
Although I'll never see it acted.
I'll hear the rain outside
And, if it's August,
A cricket's sharp chirp in the pantry.
I won't go away   *40*
Unless it rains and rains
Making the pond so large
That it joins the river,
But it never will.
I shall always sit here in this hovel
Weeping perhaps over an old Victorian novel
And hear the dingy interwinding tunes
Of country rain and wind
And lame fires of damp wood.
Especially shall I hear that starved cricket   *50*
My mind, that thinks a railway ticket
Could save it from its enclosed, cramped quality.
That mind where thoughts float round
As geese do round a pond
And never get out.

II THE SCHOOL GLOBE

Antichrist as a Child

When Antichrist was a child
He caught himself tracing
The capital letter A
On a window sill
And wondered why
Because his name contained no A.
And as he crookedly stood
In his mother's flower-garden
He wondered why she looked so sadly
Out of an upstairs window at him.   10
He wondered why his father stared so
Whenever he saw his little son
Walking in his soot-coloured suit.
He wondered why the flowers
And even the ugliest weeds
Avoided his fingers and his touch.
And when his shoes began to hurt
Because his feet were becoming hooves
He did not let on to anyone
For fear they would shoot him for a monster.   20
He wondered why he more and more
Dreamed of eclipses of the sun,
Of sunsets, ruined towns and zeppelins,
And especially inverted, upside down churches.

The Two Kites

Our kites seem
Flat fish that swim
In a high, loud river of the wind
That flows, far above us, from the lungs
Of one of the four directions.
We fly them every windy day
So that they know the North Wind's way
Of armouring all with snow and ice;
And how the South Wind
Sweet as licorice   10
Paints the summer streets of trees
With white, sweet dust;
Also they know the East Wind
That ruins the Spring;
And the West Wind whose sunset sundogs
Growl for a storm and a rainbow.

But although they wander the windy sky
Like any bird or cloud
These kites are hinged to us
Who never let them go   20
But, cruelly, must
Always pull them down
To a place where no winds blow.
How they must cry out there
Against the still, playbox air,
How they must desire to fly
Up the glass stairs of a windy sky
To where stands that cloud-nailed door
Whose doorknob sometimes is the Moon,
Whose gold latch sometimes is the Sun.   30

Those that fly kites are also kites
Carried upon a wind that comes
From nowhere,
Hurried in a direction that depends
Upon which wind of Love or Hate is blowing;
Pulled down from all our life:
Of loving, talking, singing, sighing,
Of watching the weather through windowpanes,
Of howing, hating, whethering, whying;
Pulled down from all this   40
To a grave.

Someday, for us, the Wind will stop
And, like kites, we'll listless drop,
Or a Someone will say,
"You've flown enough,
You've suffered sufficient huffpuff,"
And wind us back
To a place where no winds blow.
How we'll groan there
Against the still coffin air,   50
How we'll long to be blown
Back to the jostle of fates and plights
Of a life beneath the sun
Where the dust whirls up
Beneath the summer trees
And where every windy day,
In the bare fields, we flew our kites.

The Katzenjammer Kids

With porcupine locks
And faces which, when
More closely examined,
Are composed of measle-pink specks,
These two dwarf imps,
The Katzenjammer Kids,
Flitter through their Desert Island world.
Sometimes they get so out of hand
That a blue Captain
With stiff whiskers of black wicker   10
And an orange Inspector
With a black telescope
Pursue them to spank them
All through that land
Where cannibals cut out of brown paper
In cardboard jungles feast and caper,
Where the sea's sharp waves continually
Waver against the shore faithfully
And the yellow sun above is thin and flat
With a collar of black spikes and spines   20
To tell the innocent childish heart that
It shines
And warms (see where she stands and stammers)
The dear fat mother of the Katzenjammers.
Oh, for years and years she has stood
At the window and kept fairly good
Guard over the fat pies that she bakes
For her two children, those dancing heartaches.
Oh, the blue skies of that funny paper weather!
The distant birds like two eyebrows close together!   30
And the rustling paper roar
Of the waves
Against the paper sands of the paper shore!

The Top and the String

I wish I were a spinning top
Whipped on by a child
Whose little face was all my sky.
And I, spinning to his delight
Upon a spare room floor,
Would spin a number of times
And then be carefully
Or carelessly laid by.
The string that gave me motion
Would be put away in his pocket.   10
When he wanted me to,
I should be a gay revolver
Skipping about the floor.
Like a crazy, blue faded star
I'd run out the door
Through the bannisters
And down a pair of stairs
To where he'd find me.
But I'd not turn round forever
As I do now, day and night   20
With blood and passion's bite,
With the string of blood
Never ceasing to urge me on.
But if I were a top,
Why, the string is separate
And must be wound about me
And strongly yanked before I'll go.
The child tires of this
Or his mother and father call him away
And I have long intervals,   30
Though I'm the most furious spinning top,
Of peaceful rest, of pleasant stop.

The School Globe

Sometimes when I hold
Our faded old globe
That we used at school
To see where oceans were
And the five continents,
The lines of latitude and longitude,
The North Pole, the Equator and the South Pole—
Sometimes when I hold this
Wrecked blue cardboard pumpkin
I think: here in my hands   10
Rest the fair fields and lands
Of my childhood
Where still lie or still wander
Old games, tops and pets;
A house where I was little
And afraid to swear
Because God might hear and
Send a bear
To eat me up;
Rooms where I was as old   20
As I was high;
Where I loved the pink clenches,
The white, red and pink fists
Of roses; where I watched the rain
That Heaven's clouds threw down
In puddles and rutfuls
And irregular mirrors
Of soft brown glass upon the ground.
This school globe is a parcel of my past,
A basket of pluperfect things.   30

And here I stand with it
Sometime in the summertime
All alone in an empty schoolroom
Where about me hang
Old maps, an abacus, pictures,
Blackboards, empty desks.
If I raise my hand
No tall teacher will demand
What I want.
But if someone in authority   40
Were here, I'd say
Give me this old world back
Whose husk I clasp
And I'll give you in exchange
The great sad real one
That's filled
Not with a child's remembered and pleasant skies
But with blood, pus, horror, death, stepmothers, and lies.

Scenes for a Stereoscope

By the see-saw seashore
Walks a tall man
Who looks at the sea
And says:
Oh sea, as you forever see-saw,
Where, where is my marjorie daw?
Oh sea, with your blue
And your green rocking-horses,
Some rocking left,
Some rocking right,   10
Where, where is my marjorie daw?

Said the sea as he
Walked beside her,
Why, said she,
With a pleated shout,
Do these white hands sprout
From the shoulders of your suit?
For from the shoulders of his suit
Were sticking
A pair of white hands   20
Each one like a wing.

Oh, said he,
That was when I
Was alone in the kitchen
With the maid.
We had put our arms
Around each other
And her hands were white
With baking
And the flour came off   30
Upon my suit,

So that I went back to my wife
In the parlour
With these white hands upon my back
And my wife said, Oh Chuck,
Will you pull that blind down a trifle?
As I turned to do so like a rifle
Going off was her voice: Oh Chuck,
I see I shall have to give the maid the sack.

So he wanders in his blue serge suit   40
By the blue serge surge of the sea.
And the sea replies: Haw, haw,
You will never find your marjorie daw
But must go back to your wife
For the rest of, haw, haw, the rest of
The rest and remainder of your life.

The English Orphan's Monologue

From a slum of London,
Across thousands and thousands
Of wavy Atlantic waving waves,
I came to this farm
Where I spend servile days.
Oh, I hate these older people here
Who starch my arms and legs
With all sorts of bits and muzzles,
Saddles, steel corsets and whiffletrees.
But not my heart.   *10*
If they pinned me up as a shutter
Or with hinges made me into a door
They still could never
Bring my heart into their rule.

Sometimes at night I sit by the stove
And see the fire that is like my heart.
Like lively yellow honey is the fire
In a dead cold lion of iron;
Or like a yellow hand in Hell
Ringing an evil crackling bell;   *20*
Or like the hands of a demon gentleman
That are orange with yellow nails;
Or like a great yellow jaw
Of yellow teeth and scarlet gums;
Or like a comb, or a yellow saw.

So my heart may be sweet as honey
Though it lies in a carcass
As sullen and cold as the money
That bought that carcass;
Or my heart may be merry and gay   30
As Christmas bells of paper; or like
A greedy cruel hand that no dyke
Of morality can stop; or, sometimes,
Like a mouth howling its owner's crimes;
Or like a cruel comb or a saw is my heart.

I am the stove in which my heart hides.
Would you guess that it there resides?
No; for only at night does my heart creep out
To seduce the stupid lout
Who's the eldest boy of this family,   40
By whom I'll manage to be with child
And then they shall drive him away with me
Which is what I want.
With this heart, a fiery comb,
I'll comb your locks, Mrs.,
I'll comb Harry out of them!
And with this heart a flamey saw
I'll prune you, Mr.,
Of your nicest choicest limb.
I may seem a patient working stove   50
But inside me there's that shall shove
You all over!
Beware when that comes out!
And be sorry for every whip and clout
That you've given me.
Haw haw haw. Teeheehee.

To My Love

Sometimes I see why
People must die.
They die because they have
Too many sunsets
Stuffed into their brain.
Thousands of red and orange apples
Crowd and jostle in their mind.

But I shall not die
Although I've eaten half the stars
And the moon in all her masks   10
Of mist, dry black air,
And wind-pursued clouds;
Although my ears I've crammed
Full with the wild song of birds
Whose old music is sewed
And stitched with silver thread
Behind my eyes forever.

I shall not die
Though I have passed on winter afternoons
An empty house where someone played   20
A listless waltz upon a sad piano
And knew I should never hear
Anything as step-slowing
As that gay-gray tune again.
I shall not die
Though if I heard whoever whistled
Far away that humdrum summer afternoon,
If I heard that again
That sound should murder me.

Though down my tongue   *30*
Is thrust all sweet tastes,
Peppermint, turkish delight,
Cloves, cinnamon and honeycomb;
Though my fingers tingle
With the remembrance
Of velvet, silk, and corduroy;
Though all my senses
For essences, noises, tinkles,
The summer winds filled
With the voices of flowers   *40*
That cry for too short a season;
Though I've devoured all substance
In twenty-one years,
I shall not, must not die
Until, my Love,
Like a fantastic white glove
You my hand
(Each finger for a special sense)
Tries on
Then dig my grave   *50*
For I am ripe
For senseless, languageless lifelessness.

Dark Lagoon

Here lies the newborn child
Who, lately, lay within his mother
And stood beside a dark lagoon
Beneath a sunless, starless sky.
Great trees of thick foliage and stout trunks
Hid someone who, far away,
Seemed to be knocking out this epitaph
With muffled chisel on muffled stone:
"This child will someday die."
But these sounds came really   10
From his secret Sun,
His mother's heart that hung
Unseen in that dark sky.
The heart, whose tick-tocking
Was life to him, still prophesied
The ticking chisel of the monument-maker
As it should someday carve his name.
His mother's heart, the reason for his being,
Was yet the first clock he ever heard.

Here lies the baby innocent.   20
He is hardly as large
As the Gettysburg Address
And has never heard
The cry of "Eenie, meenie, minie, moe",
By which children choose a loser in a game,
And by which Fate seems to choose
Which children shall be which:
One-eyed, wilful, hare-lipped, lame,
Poor, orphans, idiots, or rich.
Nor has he read stories where   30
People cry, "I
Am betrayed"; a notion
That shall haunt him all his life
As also shall that dark lagoon
Where once he stood
And seemed in a grave
Though he had not yet been born;
And seemed to hear his mother's heart
Though also a clock
That with little clicking mouthfuls   40
Began to eat his time.

The Autobiography of a Marionette

This small manuscript I pen
With the quill of a furious wren.
I write this curious novel,
Within a cardboard hovel,
About my past.

When my strings were stronger
And I was very much younger
I played a primary-coloured figure
In a fairy-tale, with vigour,
And above me floated a hand-shaped cloud   10
From which a strict, white rain fell loud
Of strings,
Strings that made marionette marry marionette,
Or laugh, or lie, or scream, or beget,
Or waltz, or weep, or die, or foxtrot
Through many a hollow, cardboard grot.
There were dialogues
With golliwogs
And public school
And high school.   20

In that continual rain
That poured from those distant hands
There came fates, of pleasure or pain,
That tied us with steely bands
To a life where we were a vase of foottracks.
All these footsteps must be spilt out,
Each one shaped like a trout,
Before in Death's cardboard coffin we'd relax.

III THE GREAT LAKES SUITE

Bodies of Fresh Water

I Lake Superior

I am Lake Superior
Cold and gray.
I have no superior;
All other lakes
Haven't got what it takes;
All are inferior.
I am Lake Superior
Cold and gray.
I am so cold
That because I chill them   10
The girls of Fort William
Can't swim in me.
I am so deep
That when people drown in me
Their relatives weep
For they'll never find them.
In me swims the fearsome
Great big sturgeon.
My shores are made of iron
Lined with tough, wizened trees.   20
No knife of a surgeon
Is sharper than these
Waves of mine
That glitter and shine
In the light of the Moon, my mother
In the light of the Sun, my grandmother.

II Lake Michigan

For I'm a michigoose
And he's a michigander: Old Vaudeville Song

By the shores of Lake Michigan,
Chicago sits
Filled with jawbreakers
Filled with lawbreakers.

By the shores of Lake Michigan,
Lives the Michigander,
Lives the Michigoose.
Very silly people they
For they had the nerve to say
When they used to visit us   10
In the days of yore,
"That the Yankees,
The Yankees won the war!"

"Bah!" said we
Patriotically.
"How your wits do wander
You Michigoose, you Michigander!"
Right then and there we had a fight
With our cousins from Michigan
Who shortly after went back there again.   20
And since we won, we knew we were right.

74

III *Lake Huron*

Yoohoo Yoohoo
I'm blue, blue
Lake Huron.
By my shores
In fratricidal wars
Indians killed each other.
At Bayfield
The people stop
To see me slop
Against the pier.   10
At Grand Bend
The people tend
Instead to
Look at each other.
The Au Sable River and the Maitland
Flow into me.
They think I'm a sea
But haw haw
They're not through yet
For blue and wet   20
I flow into Lake St. Clair
And Lake St. Clair into Lake Erie
So very very weary
And Lake Erie into
Lake Ontario
Like a blue grain bag
At which that frowsy hag
Of a city Toronto nibbles.
And then the River St. Lawrence!
Whose waters resemble those   30
Dark barrelled waves that
Drowned the Duke of Clarence.
So haw haw you Maitland River
And you Au Sable one too.
For when you flow into me
You're not at all through.

IV *Lake St. Clair*

I once knew a bear
Who swam in Lake St. Clair
And after the experience
Said, "Hoity Toit
I don't like the way Detroit
Pollutes the air there."
Then after a while
He added with a smile,
"And I don't like the way Windsor
Does, either."   10

V *Lake Erie*

Lake Erie is weary
Of washing the dreary
Crowds of the cities
That line her shores.
Oh, you know
The dirty people of Buffalo
And those in Cleveland
That must leave land
To see what the water's like.
And those that by bike,   10
Motorcar, bus and screeching train
Come from London in the rain
To Port Stanley where they spend
The day in deciding whether Grand Bend
Might not have been a nicer place to go.

Up and down in thousands
They walk upon Lake Erie's sands.
Those in Cleveland say, "Plainly,"
As they gaze across the waters
Where swim their sons and daughters,   20
"That distant speck must be Port Stanley."
Those in Port Stanley yawn, "Oh,
That lump in the mist
Over there really must
Be populous Cleveland in Ohio."
But Lake Erie says, "I know
That people say I'm shallow
But you just watch me when I go
With a thump
And a plump   30
At the Falls of Niagara into Lake Ontario.
When you see that you'll admit
That I am not just a shallow nitwit
But a lake
That takes the cake
For a grand gigantic thunderous tragic exit."

VI Lake Ontario

Left! Right! march the waves
Towards the sandy shore
Where I stand and motionless
Stare at their blue roar.
Oh, they would stop and listen
And be my blue audience
If I could leap and glisten
More than they, more than they.
But although within me rush
Waves Death cannot deny   10
I must upon these coasts
Only listen to their cry.
My voice is soft while theirs is loud,
Loud their wavy boasts
That do drown out all reply.
I am one, they are a crowd.
Yet though I'm still and alone
Upon these thin saltless sands,
Thousands only shall hear the waves
Clap their fresh young hands   20
In lawless blue applause,
Because I held a megaphone
To their blue green blue noise,
Because I made this seashell,
This poem, for your ear,
My dear Monseer,
Of their blue continual hell.

Grand Bend

It is the rutting season
At Grand Bend
And the young men and the women
Explode in each other's arms
While no chaperons attend.
By this furious activity
Of the loin
No children are conceived
For they have avoided this.
While the sun   10
Sprays everyone with iodine
And old men sit
Upon the dirty beach
With great bellies big
Not with child
But with creamed asparagus.
And to somewhat more disgust
Someone has spilt a bottle of scent.
Crazily the cheap sweetness
Leaps through the air   20
Making some think of something decaying
And others of stenographers in the rain
And another to say giddily,
"How violent, at Grand Bend this year,
How violent the violets are!"

Niagara Falls

When the bridegroom
Reaches the room
With breath bated
He approaches
The moment long awaited.
He takes off his loud cravat
And his shirt and his hat,
His trousers and his shoes,
And his undershirt and drawers.
Naked, as from his mother,   10
He attempts with another
To return to that sweet night of the womb.

IV THE IVORY STEEPLE

The Ivory Steeple

O proletariat I weep for you!
For your appalling working conditions
For the hole in your shoe.
All my gloves and shoes
Are invisibly mended and holeless
But that is no reason why yours should be.
You really wouldn't be any different
If you were richer
And I don't feel at all that you're submerged.
You make an interesting wallpaper   10
For my peculiar blessedness.
I can giggle at you reading the funny papers
While I peruse the works of Cyril Tourneur.
You read such things as *Handy Andy*
While I (for the fourth time) *Tristram Shandy.*
Oh hawwhawwheeheehahahawwhaww haw hoon you.
And as I can afford my hot water bottles and incense,
A Christmas rose on the window sill,
7 pairs of brown oxfords and 4 of black,
Recordings of Stravinsky (like monstrous sea-shells)   20
Singing of seas (blue hands slapping blue faces)
Or Beckford's *Vathek*
Or the committing of a delicate original sin
Or reading the latest collection of Anais Nin,
Your pinched white and gray faces
Peer in
Like small white tracts held off at a distance.
Well . . . is it not all very beautiful?
As you stand hungry in the rain
Just look to what heights you too may attain.   30

The Orphanage

We are orphans
And gleam
In our yellow dresses
(The yellow of a twenty-watt light-bulb)
Like a piece of coloured fan-light.
They lit this dingy flame
(These yellow dresses)
They that lie pasted together
In ditches by the railroad tracks
And seethe in round-shouldered cars   10
With the lusty belches of a Canadian spring.
Young men with permanent waves
Crawl over ghastly women
Whose cheeks are fat as buttocks.
Young men who play hockey
On frozen milk
And ride motorcycles
(Their horses drink the green blood of ancient ferns)
Come out to abandoned orchards
With girls   20
Who have not read Baudelaire
Or anything.

Miss Mumblecrust
Wears earrings
Like scimitars
Swinging at her ears
Swishing and cutting
Imaginary grass.

She loves
And her mouth waters   30
For the hard caramel bellies
Of young men
Who play hockey in winter.
The parts in their hair
Are like pink worms
That crawl towards us.

At night
They say
Men and women
Fit together   40
Among the elderly trees.
It is they who kindle
The yellow of our dresses.
We are the answers
To those equations
In ditches and round-shouldered cars.
And gray windows
Bob with plain white
And cretinous faces.

A Miscellany

I

What a hero I am,
Said Nero to his dam.
Yes, precious, replied she,
You're a regular epitome
Of what one ought not to be
To be a hero.
Not, did you say, mama?
No, dear, ought.

II

You bore me, said a young ninny,
With a very lipstick-clogged whinny,
To Jane Austen.
I rather think, said the author of Emma,
That I would,
And that it is, my dear, your dilemma!

III

Said the famous Vienna physician,
I have operated
On many a metaphysician
And not found
(This is unkind)
Soul or Mind!

IV

God made us in his image
Only duller
As a reflection's so
In ditch-water
Or dish-water.

We have made God in our image
Only brighter;
What one wishes
When one wishes to be good
Only righter.   10

Klaxon

All day cars mooed and shrieked,
Hollered and bellowed and wept
Upon the road.
They slid by with bits of fur attached,
Fox-tails and rabbit-legs,
The skulls and horns of deer,
Cars with yellow spectacles
Or motorcycle monocle,
Cars whose gold eyes burnt
With a too-rich battery,   10
Murderous cars and manslaughter cars,
Chariots from whose foreheads leapt
Silver women of ardent bosom.
Ownerless, passengerless, driverless,
They came to anyone
And with headlights full of tears
Begged for a master,
For someone to drive them
For the familiar chauffeur.
Limousines covered with pink slime   20
Of children's blood
Turned into the open fields
And fell over into ditches,
The wheels kicking helplessly.
Taxis begged trees to step inside
Automobiles begged of posts
The whereabouts of their mother.
But no one wished to own them any more,
Everyone wished to walk.

Rewards for Ambitious Trees

Fame to trees may come
Through at last advancing
On the savage dunce
Who counts the syllables of time
In the castle near Dunsinane.
Some achieve the wearing of a young lady
Who is pursued in her farthingale
By a hot rash ravisher.
She clings like a pink wrist-watch
Imploring one to be hollow.   10
Some are very old
Or are planted by Bismarck
Or caught Wordsworth's eye.
Victory falls to those
That fall on people
Or kill a longhaired prince.
Some prophesy with wooden scream
The wicked farmer's death
The sunk sun
The fallen star   20
The rumpled nebulae . . . .

The Coffins

These coffins are submarines
That will sail beneath the slopes
Of gray-green old graveyards.

One white lone sailor to each
Submarine that navigates
The wormy seas of earth.

With shrouds for uniforms
Stitched by weeping tailors
These bony sailors
Shall sail deep field and morass   10
Without periscope or compass
They'll only dimly know
That someday they must flow
Into the final harbour
On some high gray shore
Where the Lord shall weigh
Men's wicked souls on Doomsday.

The Groats

Oh the wasps and the bees
That are furry as yellow and black
Fat sofas and chesterfields
Suck at the groats,
Or butterflies listen there
To their Master's voice
For there is a gramaphone
Of choir-boys
Hidden at their roots,
Or the Italian humming-bird   10
Pierces with thin black rapier
Into their ivory ears.

Dream Within Dream

I slept and dreamed
A collection of dreams
That fitted each into each other
Like the dungeons and cells
Of a great dark jail.
Dreamed! rode pillion rather
With a demon in front of me
Upon a horse whose favourite hay
Was human hair.
Dream within dream dreamt I.   10
I dreamt a dream in which I woke
And, when awake, I killed a man.
Then, still in this dream, I fell asleep
And dreamt again that I woke
And pushed a woman over a cliff.
Next I choked a vivacious gentleman;
Then I stabbed a girl on an ottoman.
Each time the face cf the man became
More like my father's face;
And that of the woman, of course,   20
Began to seem like my mother's,
As if I could have slain my parents
For that foul deed that struck
Me out of chaos, out of nothing.

At last I swam out of my nightmare
And managed to pray to Heaven
With its thousand white stars
To somehow stop my maddened mind
From making the reflection
Of reflection of my bad despair.   30
So then I dreamt my last dream.
I dreamt I was the bed
I slept upon and, lifeless, cared
Not what sack of blood and bones,
What pillar of dust
Made my springs creak
Or weighed me down.
At last I woke!

The Beauty of Miss Beatty

The beauty of Miss Beatty,
As everyone declared,
Was the way her bosoms dared
Though never really bared
To seem so anyhow.
Though some shrieked,
How like a cow!
And others uttered to their mother,
Not a bosom but an udder!
Oh, what a snake, what an adder she is!   *10*
For see how all, ALL, the men
Even those with a wen
Or a hump
Or a lump
On the back of their necks
Or with only one arm
Like a pump
Flock around her
In a great clump
Ever at her beck and call to flounder   *20*
In the great glittering puddle of her charm!

Oh, look, said the Mother
Oh, look ahead, said she,
To her rather plain daughter.
Look ahead
To the beauty of Miss Beatty in her grave.
Death is notoriously bored with bosoms
And touches them and punctures them
Without any compunction.
He topples over the tent   *30*
Sucks at and withers it
And as you know my dear
And as everyone certainly ought to
It has always been that lust
Has always rhymed with dust.

88

A Fantasy and a Moral

Fantasy
By the moon's rented light,
By that silver secondhand sun
That seems like all remembered things,
She could be seen
As she lay in her dark bedroom
Asleep and naked.
The darkness enclosed her
As a dark sock contains a white guitar
Or a black cloud extinguishes a brilliant star.

Now her breasts like two balloons   10
Draw her forth to wicked forests.
For they swell till they lift her
Up out of her bed, out of her room,
Through the door, down a stairs,
And into the fields of night
Where, above,
The silly piebald half-moon,
Out of breath
And frightened to death,
Half-white, half-black,   20
Sidles and slides across the dark floor
Where clouds are rowing with windy oar.

Low over the ground she floats
Until she reaches a grave grove
Where down winding paths she flows.
There a fox leaps up at her
In angry hunger
And luna-moths whose eyes resemble
Tears in a sunset
About her tumble and noctambulate.   30

Into a thicket of Jack-in-the-Pulpit plants
She does finally descend
And hears not one of those sly sermons
With which Reverend Jack catches flies,
For fiends dart forth
And upon her execute such actions
That thresh nervous drops of dew
Down from all leaves and twigs about her.

In the morning
She awakes in a garden near her house   40
While in the West as soft as a mouse
The moon is hurrying away
Before the sun shall rise.
Flowers surround her
As she wonders at her sleep-walking
And remembers a dream
Where a gentleman kissed her
And promised her his love beneath a tree
And said she was a hand
And he her glove,   50
So fitted were they to each other.
How wittily, how nicely he put it!
She never notes how sly
Her breasts look.
They should indeed look sly
For they have floated and lifted her
To a demon's love
Whose poisonous child she'll bear and die.

Moral
So love, though measured breath by breath,
May seem like walking in a summer dream,   60
Visiting nowhere but pleasant places;
So love does often lead a filthy way to Death.

Coffins

Coffins are Death's eggs
Whose yolks, then, are the corpses
Of dead men and women,
Girls, boys and babies,
Girlfriends, boyfriends and lovers.
Death lays them in her cold nest
That is the gravelly ancient breast
Of Earth, that rotting head
That like a criminal's face
Severed and thrown from the block   10
Tumbles round and round
The pitying merciful Sun.

And Death, her children laid
(With Abel as her nest-egg),
Then waits for them to hatch
Upon the branches of a dead tree
Which neither wind nor rain
Can strike down or revive.
She waits, oh centuries! in vain
For never will the pharaoh hid   20
In secret room within the pyramid
Rise for her from his golden bed
Until Queen Death herself is dead.

The Chough

The chough, said a dictionary,
Is a relation of the raven
And a relative of the crow.
It's nearly extinct,
But lingers yet
In the forests about Oporto.
So read I as a little child
And saw a young Chough in its nest,
Its very yellow beak already tasting
The delicious eyes   10
Of missionaries and dead soldiers;
Its wicked mind already thinking
Of how it would line its frowsy nest
With the gold fillings of dead men's teeth.
When I grew older I learned
That the chough, the raven and the crow
That rise like a key signature of black sharps
In the staves and music of a scarlet sunset
Are not to be feared so much
As that carrion bird, within the brain,   20
Whose name is Devouring Years,
Who gobbles up and rends
All odds and ends
Of memory, good thoughts and recollections
That one has stored up between one's ears
And whose feet come out round either eye.

The Oracular Portcullis

Illyria's hair fell down
Like a long golden answer
To a question in long division.
Gradually she let her saucer down
Crushing the invisible column
Of time and space beneath
Into a gently wounded saucer
And slowly the white portcullis rose,
The cruel ivory portcullis of her mouth
That had closed on both victims and visitors: 10
Many poached eggs and pieces of toast,
Duchess of Oldenburg apples,
And oceans of broth and soup.
Slowly Illyria made
Her delirious epigram:
"It is surely a well-known fact,
My dear,
That women are concave,
And men are convex?"
Thus spake Illyria; this question she posed,   20
Then quite quickly her portcullis closed.

The Death of the Poetess

Her collected works
Published at last
Alas just before.
Here are the 32
Little white grave-stones
Engraved on both sides
With epitaphs.
She was a spire that dreams
In a rocking-chair
Or a spire laid sideways   10
On a sofa.
A spire that sipped tea,
A soft pink spire.
In her illness
Books fell from her bed
Like heavy marble leaves
(As they fall in Vallombrosa)
From a marble tree.
Now the clock that is her heart
Tick-tocks itself to stop.   20
Beside her corpse
Lies the Collected Edition
32
Thin gravestones.

A Riddle

We need no gloves,
Our hands englove each other.
We need no scarves,
Our arms that purpose serve.
We need no trousers,
No overcoats, no hats.
Ourselves do clothe each other
Fully against all cold, wind and rain.
What are we
Who need no raiment   10
Nor the help of weavers, hatters,
Tailors, milliners, stitchers, glovers,
To whom no winter matters?
Answer: A pair of very loving lovers.

The Bird of Paradise

The bird of Paradise fades
And gray grows the Ace of Spades.
Cracked is the once loud bell
And low fall the fires of Hell.

The bird of Paradise, when wet
With dew, seemed a flying sunset;
And the Ace of Spades was blacker
Than a negro dipped in lacquer.
The bell summoned some to Heaven,
Told others it was half past eleven.   10
The fires of Hell burnt a swarm of sinners,
In their heyday, and all the winners
Of bets on horses and sweepstakes, tch!
Tch! So my tongue like the wick
Of a lamp shall someday fail
Of any glinting words and pale
Shall falter with a sigh and pout
That all Fire, all Hell, all Poetry is out.

3 POEMS 1951–60

In This Round Place

Every thing in this round place,
This round blue head we live in,
Everything is mysterious, far
And unnameable;
Far from explaining, far from capture
In the trap of a tongue in a face.

In this curved place He sent us to,
The curved mind cannot tell
Why the moon should fit the sun
In eclipses, or why do   10

Some flowers take the colour of Mars
Or clouds like summer milk seem.
What can the detective know for sure
In his hunt for the reason
Of a winter season
Or of whirlwinds and falling stars.

The whirlwind, the rainbow and the star
That falls like a golden shoelace,
For them and the poison
That damns the white mushroom   20
None knows what the reasons are.

Why do the birds sing like silver hinges
To the doors of Heaven,
Why does the bread rise like a ghost
From the grave of its oven,
Why does the wind blow with such voice
As grief is given,
Why do the clouds so lowly move
Like the souls of our grandfathers
Bringing us rain in their love.   30

99

The dust that hangs
In the air of a room
Teaches astronomers humble comparisons,
The faces on dusty floors
Teach us unsureness and hesitations
For we like a Jack in the box
In our small air
Like a thought in a skull
Think we spiral when we straight line
Think we are spoon when we're forktine   **40**
And cannot explain why hair
Can be cut with a knife, so certain
Are we of the place where we're hid
When of our coffin we have not discovered
The doomsday to open lid
Nor have found yet
That to open the eye is to shut an eye
For in those opened seeing places
Blindness, and more closed eyelids lie.

Like twelve rocking chairs   **50**
Rocking on top of each other
With you, the eye, the I in the twelfth,
So difficult is the riddle
Why all the fingerprints are different
And who is our mother
Why, why we are here sent
And where is the middle.

1951

The Tall Black Hat

As a child, I dreamt of tomorrow
Of the word "tomorrow" itself.
The word was a man in a tall black hat
Who walked in black clothes through
Green fields of quiet rain that
Beneath gray cloudfields grew.

Tall as trees or Abraham Lincoln
Were that man's brothers
Who when they become To-day
Die and dissolve one by one   10
Like licorice morning shadows
When held in the mouth of the sun.

Yesterday is an old greataunt
Rocked off in her rocking chair
To cellars where old light and snow
And all yesterdays go;
To-day was a small girl bringing
China cupfuls of water and air
And cages of robins singing,
"It is positively no crime   20

To have pleasure in Present Time."
But Tomorrow is most impressive
Like the hired man back from the fair
He comes to the child still sleeping
With pockets of longer hair,
A handful of longer fingers
And the Indian I remember
At dusk, crossing Market Square.

The man in the tall black hat
Brought the gipsy who was drunk   30
And the white faced cat
Who stepped before my stepmother
The very first time she came.

He gave the child a yellow leaf,
He holds the arrow for my heart,
He dropped the playing card in the lane,
He brought the dancing weasel,
And the old man playing the jewsharp.

101

He brings the wind and the sun
And the stalks of dead teazle   40
Seen on a windless winter walk,
He fetches a journey's direction
From his garden of weathervanes
And mines, like diamonds, the tears
For the glittering windowpanes
Of rain and sorrow.

All the days of all the years
The dark provider hunts me
Whom I named Sir Thomas Tomorrow
After my dream of him,   50
And in the grave fields of mystery
This black man has brothers
Who have followed him and come
Ever since with all I must see,
With Earth, Heaven and the tenor drum
I played in the C.O.T.C.,
The sound of bells and stars in a tree
Are stuck to their thumb
And lie in their tall black hats and pockets
Like pictures in locked and closed lockets.   60

At midnight he knocked and arrived
As the old woman really rocked away
And he took off his tall hat which
Changed into a small white cup,
White as the new light of day.
To the girl as small as a switch,
The girl who wakes me up,
His tallness and blackness shrank
To leave behind on the floor
From his pockets of come to pass   70
Puzzles and lonely birds to see
Diamonded names upon window glass,
A whistle, a straw and a tree.

But see out where small in the dawn
Through the hanging wingflash dance
Of the little flies, the wrens and the doves
Who are the seconds and minutes and hours
Floating over the acres of distance,
See his brother with feet of slate
Begin to walk through the wet flowers   80
Towards me with his speck of Future
And a tall black hatful of Fate.

1952

102

The Table of Dishes

I saw in my dream a farmer's wife
Set a table with empty dishes
On a mourning early November evening.
The light came through rain and from the stove
As she went out of the kitchen to get something.
Then it happened that the dishes talked
And did such things as you now will hear.

   * * *

Up jumped the cups, led by one old unhandled one.
Well, sang they, without us they could not get
Their tea so their mouths could be wet.   10
We have touched all their mouths; they all
Have drunk from us here, for ten miles around
At funerals and weddings: thus the cups sang,
Continuing thus while with heavier voice
Came six old worn white plates' honest cries
As they wheeled recklessly about:
Upon us do they look for their meat,
Upon us is it carefully laid down.
We, flat and smooth, hold it still for them.
We are the dish of their fatness and leanness   20
With our faithful flat old hands we shout.
Then an earthenware milk pitcher said she was sacred.
For she was the holder of white milk and life.
Then up jumped an aged soup tureen
Holloing and bellowing his giant responsibility.
The meat platter, the potato dish, the bread plate,
All sang of their happiness in service;
The knives, forks and spoons ringing bell-like
In silver quarrelings of who did most,
The whole kitchen filled with unseen, half-seen   30
Boastings, jumping up and downs of kettles, ovens,
Of lids, jars, ladles, pans, sieves and graters,
Basins, dippers, sifters, pots, dampers, lifters, pokers,
All the utensils in that darkening kitchen who
Considered their goodness, their civilization,
Their speechless, silent holding together of people,
Eating and drinking around a table.

   * * *

So they sang and danced not forgetting the grief
Of cups and dishes that break, for one broken thing
Is one less thing to carry the world's nursing nourishment,
One less handy cup to carry the water to the dying man's mouth,
One more step near the lapping beast's water reflection.
Up they whirled, thus singing, rejoicing, in one
Flashing earthenware white china moon shape,
Hollow, a revolving great cup made of mad dishes,
One huge grail ready for a simple lord's supper,
The oil cloth tablecloth swooping up
For the dishes its hollow to rest in,
Till the door opens and the farmer's wife
Comes up from the cellar with eggs and with meat.

    * * *

Oh, still table of empty set dishes, ready for six persons
To sit down and from you eat their daily bread.
Simple saucer and plain cup, holy and holder,
Quiet hands that proffer the fruits of the earth.
Oh to hold you, to hold that blessed pitcher
Whose blood, poured out,
Feeds hundreds of the poor, the lost, and thousands of the hungry,
The farmer, the toiler, the mouths old Adam's Curse
Opened in this great dish of Earth.

1953

The Horn

What is the horn that the dawn holds,
A soft shrill horn of feathers,
Cold as the dew on the grass by the paths,
Warm as the fire in the match in the box.
When this horn blows, in a sky of the sun
There rises our green star of earth
And the four evangelists who've borne
Thy bed down through the night
Now leave thee still thine eyes to see
The sun's separation of shadows.   10

Neither capons nor pullets nor hens
Can wake the sun and the world;
Only the prophets of the Old Testament
Huge old cocks, all speckled and barred,
Their wings like ragged pages of sermons,
Only they from their roosts in the henhouse
Can rouse the bread from its oven-sleep,
Raise the smoke from the haunted chimney.

Fierce old cock whose eyes look blind
So glaring and inspired are they,   20
Who live in this dungeon of cramp and dirt;
Fierce old fowl with shaking red wattles
Surrounding a beak like a kernel of wheat,
A yellow beak, plump, twisted and sharp
Which opens, hinged and prizing cry,
To show the sun's fistful of golden darts.

1953

Jordan

Clouds cross Jordan every day.
I see them disappear that way.
I press against the walls of sky,
The walls of ground and of my
Five slow senses that still meet
Only a muck beneath my feet
That's Jordan's shore but not its tide.

Who cross to the other side
Brighter than the sun become.
Trumpet, harp flute fiddle and drum   *10*
Do they play there in their dancing
Nearer with their psalms advancing,
Like the leaning summer earth,
Nearer the source of all their mirth.
Then they move back to rest from joy
Lest sameness delight destroy
With sounds of cloud, rain and seas
And winter winds through hollow trees.

When will my slow stars allow
Fulfillment of this longing vow?   *20*
I walk through holy Bible land
Blazing martyrs in my hand
Yet in learned illiteracy
Just bare letters can I see.
Yes, His spouting Dove may I get
And cannot be one drop wet.

Still I know that when not praying
Bible and candle will float by,
Water at knee and thigh not staying
But to chest and head now fly,   *30*
Widening eyes till they see
The golden world about that Tree
Adam saw once to disappear
Since then until recovery here.

1956

The Windyard

I built a windyard for the wind;
  The wind like a wild vast dog came up
To play with weathervanes and corners
  My keyholes and my chinks.

And for the sea I built a well;
  The brookish tomcat gurgled in,
Waterfell and sprung about
  Hunting throats and boots.

I stood a house up for the earth;
  The mappy girl came in   10
With rut and footstep path
  That wind the traveller up.

A stove I hammered for the sun;
  In flew the golden oriole
To crackle sticks of time
  And sing the loaves of space.

Come girl well yard and stove,
  Come Flesh Heart Mind and Lyre,
Come Earth Water Wind and Fire.   20
        Well, when they came
Barking, meowing, talking and caroling,
I stepped above both house and yard
        Into myself.

1956

107

The Marble Windbreaker

All that the mind can think of:
Things like chimneys in swimming,
Owls in cahoots, "upon the pond",
New incests, marble windbreakers,
Animals that are extinct
Because they never were
"Allowed & loud, upset & downset";
That the act of sexual union is but a symbol,
Suspects the most hideous things of splendid people,
Wants to draw faces with ears for eyes . . .   10
Dative trees and accusative lawyers,
"The werewolves were whining",
"Deathcries and birthrattles",
"Latvia me do this, the Would Pile,
I watercan & first of May do it;
I shall go & Eye shallow ghoul",
Subordinate cats with subordinate claws,
In short
All the things, for example, that the mind can think of.

1956

Writing and Loving

Grammar's mistake is Love's correctness:
She likes the fused sentence, the commafault kiss,
Abhors loving the interior of one's clothes, the period,
The colon, the semicolon . . . bars to conjunction.

The periodic sentence definites the usually indefinite
Article; the paratactic she-sentence, with her verb
At the beginning & 1000's of modifiers after,
Spreads wide her subordinate clauses & colours
His infinitive with her introductory modifier
Until after some careful parallelism,   10
Slowly breaking into phrases, words mere
Letters of the alphabet until a blank page of ecstasy.

1956

108

The Sparrow

His feathers are the dark subway
Dripping with train oil and rain
His voice is the funny squeak chalk
That draws the obscene twain
Ogre and ogress eight feet long:
Sing their wedding, ding dung
        Ding dung chirp chirp
Underneath the timely thunder of the trains.

Beneath the level of the street
In a grotto of frozen stale urine   10
Stand the gods of stolen chalk
Scoured by the tunnel wind;
Trains and cars and feet and bicycles
Dance above the waiting festering dolls:
Sing sparrows at their wedding
        Ding dung, cheep cheep cheep cheep
The old newspapers fly up like jangled brains.

Speculation seizes on the possibility
Of lights flaring wherever these are worshipped.
How many times here? Once for a certainty   20
In the episcopal garage; hark, the city's glowing—
An intense white light for animals, blue for
Paederasts, purple for nocturnal effusions, for
Onan a green light and yellow for the normal.
        Hymen Sparrow, bring the torches:
Clatter clatter clatter clatter
        Chirp chirp ding dung bell
I walked through the city lit by love.

Dirty, diseased, impish, unsettling, rapist
Illegitimate, urban, southless, itching,   30
Satyromaniac, of butcher string the harpist,
The sparrows and their gods are everything.
I like to hear their lack of tune
On a very cold winter snowy afternoon.
They must be listened to and worshipped each—
The shocking deities: ding dung is sacred
        So is filthiness, obscenity
            Chirp, chirp.
Even whores can on occasion muster up a grail.

Christ and Gautama and Emily Brontë were   40
Born in the midst of angelic whir
In a dripping concrete den under,
Under the alimentary trains: it is we
Who see the angels as brown lechery
And the sacred pair—Venus and Adonis
As automatons coupled as a train is.
        And so step down my chalky reader,
            Why keep our festival here
                In this crotch?
            Ding dung chirp chirp: 50
A sparrow sings if you but have an ear.

1958

The Hummingbird

The hum of an approaching christening mob!
The hanging still in the air with so much motion
He flies with wings of air in an air of feathers!
The hanging still in the air with so much motion

The hollow twig that transports flowers to his blood
The barn of flowers pressed in a jumping ounce
No song is needed when one is a song
The barn of flowers pressed in a jumping ounce

Enoch, Elijah or Ascension is your name
My dainty jaunt, why call I you these names?   10
Because I realize and advertise that there
Far down the dark row of mountains cowering
That ruby flash that is the chariot of fire
        Is your throat too.

1958

Doomsday, or the Red Headed Woodpecker

I
    Red Sky!
    Morning!
Shaking like a scarlet head!
    Doomsday!
    Rise up!
Spring your lids, you dead!
    Scrape out
    Coffins!
Put yourself together!
    Pat that dust!   10
    Find that bust!
This is the last weather!
    Trumpet!
    Drummer!
    Thunder!
Vomit you cannibals!
    Shake out those
    Those old flesh dresses
For the resurrection parties and balls!

II
Here comes St. Sebastian with a handful of arrows!   20
  The big threshing woodpecker is
  Beating on the green drum!
Here comes the poor boy who got caught in the harrows!
Here comes St. Bartholomew with his skin!
      Scroll away!
      Hell this way!
      Heaven that!
      Rat a tat tat!
There goes Death and there goes Sin!
  Here come Cain and Abel   30
      Hand in hand!
Here come horizontals pursued by slopes,
      Here comes a table
    Changing back to a tree and
Here come the hanged people skipping with their ropes!

III
    Red Sky!
    Morning!
Shaking like a scarlet head!
    Doomsday!
    Rise up!   40
Spring your lids, you dead!
    Scrape out
    Coffins!
Put yourself together!
    Pat that dust!
    Find that bust!
This is the last weather!
    Trumpet!
    Drummer!
    Thunder!   50
Vomit you cannibals!
    Shake out those
    Those old flesh dresses
For the resurrection parties and balls!

1958

The Morning Dew

Shake seed of light and thunder
From where you hang,
The Word without the Flesh.

The pastures, sloughs and trees all shine
Their leaves and grasses sown
With flashing tears.

Here is Absalom's hair in crystal terms
Feverish bonfire of the sensual body,
Bloodbob.

Sharp, sharp yellow teeth, sharp sharp   10
In the dark mouth blinking of the
Fox-haired queen.

Blue as the fields of flax in the summer
That dream of retting, spreading, drying,
White linen snow.

Green as the thoughtful ancient woods
Ash contemplation of linden tree thinking,
Paththrough.

The killdeer's nest is built of gold,
Cobwebs are blessed and Eden   20
Has caught these fields within her fold.

1958

114

The Executioner of Mary Stuart

There was a jolly headsman once
Attached to an ancient castle.
They chose him specially for his task—
    To murder other rascals.

For example I have often felt
My analogy might be
A rat-trap made from the bones of rats
    And that was simple old me.

So my life was ruined but I
Was given a sort of reward: 10
The clothes of the executed,
    Often some astonishing rich brocade.

One day I caught in my jaws
A woman who dazzled the sun.
I chopped off her head as my task
    And took what was left for my fun.

Annunciation to the Mud
In the beginning was the Dark
Bridegroom to a headless Queen,
    Far off I hear the hell dogs bark.   20

1958

The Yellow-Bellied Sapsucker

I

    The terrifying form of the pebble,
    The awful hieroglyph of the dewdrop,
    The obscure character of the ravelled string,
    The mysterious letter of the bent straw,
    The teeming message of the dead groundhog,
The difficult sentence of the old beggar with two canes,
And the whore on Yonge Street with her stockings rolled down,
        Such a suffix hard to render:
The untranslatable participles of the rushing wind,
The gentle telegram in a dank code from the firefly swamp,   10
    The golden feather on the path through the bush
        That flew a song in a lost language.

II

    The pebble towered dark and purple over me,
    The dewdrop made me doubt my value,
    The ravelled string hanged me with despair,
    There was no lexicon for the straw letter,
    The groundhog's sea of worms sickened,
The two caned sentence disappeared down the road,
The short runty cabbie on his night off picked her up,
The dead leaves, the lightning, the thunder and the rainbow   20
    Sailed away with the wind but I didn't,
    The blinking swamp led me muddy nowhere,
And the feather, it was just a feather, nothing but.

III

Came Christ the Tiger and Buddha the Balloon
Hercules the Lion and Bacchus the Drunkard
Emily the Prostitute of Snow, and Dame Trot
Sly Tod, Reverend Jones, Kitty Cradle
Baby Cobbler with his Rattle Sparkler
Mad William Lyon with his bastard and Blake
With his trained angels, Spenser with his   30
Creepyland, Shakespeare with his no-handed Lavinia,
St. John with the Seven Days wound up,
Nothing left but miles of Sabbath,
Solomon who sang of his foot in the doorway,
Gorgeous salesman, Sterne with his
Involved snigger: came Love, Innocence,
Rainbow, Whirlwind and Falling Star.

IV

          And then
The pebble was a mountain that took years to climb
The dewdrop was all reality itself   40
The string was the pathway to Heaven
The straw formed God's name
The groundhog meant that Death was laughter
The old beggar with the sack on his back
Was God the Father bearing up his creation
With Adam and Eve the two canes before him,
To what journey's end? perhaps some hayloft
With the rain beating down on the owly roof.
The Whore was the Holy Ghost herself,
"The dearling noursling of his bosome," Sophia,   50
Who told him how to make it all "at her behest."
    The wind was the world of words, all poetry
      At its giant blind Pentecostal source,
The nine mused and pleated winnowing fan of wisdom,
The fireflies led me to Noah's Ark,
    And the golden feather sang:

V

          Existence has a yellow belly
            And sucks sap
    It pecks life in a dead tree.
    It is a boyish drummer   60

    Who takes the stick of life
       So powerful
    And takes that fork's wife
    So wise, the spoon of death

    And beats out upon the drum
    Of the third state, the other room
    Rented to both right and wrong
    To both death and life . . . Eternity!

    Eternity, that drum, sang the bird.
    Play on it with life and with death!   70

VI
        The scene changes:
The mountain is a pebble in your hand
The abyss of Space is a dewdrop
        Heaven Road lies ravelled in your pocket
        Time's cloud of moments is a rain drop
          On the fence,
        God lies even in our excrement
        What Bible says, a groundhog babbles too,
        A passerby is the Creator
The holy Ghost is your wife or husband,   80
        Shakespeare, your whistle,
And the thousand eyes of fancy make each idle stare
        Possible breakthrough to the perfect.

VII
        Golden Feather
        Of the yellow bellied sapsucker
        You are a golden spring
        A golden voice
        A golden tree and a golden torch
By whose light and in whose world
I show all complexity unfurled.   90

1959

Rachel

I
When I was a young man
    Passing the city dump
In the smoking rubbish I heard
    A small and rusty wail.

      Naked
    Unwashed from the caul
    Thy navel string uncut
A crusted, besmattered and loathsome thing.

I fouled my clothes and stank
    But I brought you to my house.   10
I found that your mother was a gypsy,
    Your father an Indian.

But "Live!" I said, and you lived.
    You grew like a field of flax,
Your hair was gold as the sun,
    Your breasts were blossoms.

I walked by your foster house,
    It was the time of love.
I rewarded your governess for
    Pearly runs in your Scarlatti.   *20*

II
It was the time of love
I was so afraid you'd say no
My heart beat like giant footsteps
I felt agony in your garden.

    Again you came to my house,
I was ashamed to ask you so often,
    I gave you a golden ring
        And a glass pen.

    You dressed in silk
    You bathed in milk   *30*
    But as we embraced
On your shoulder I saw the red speck.

    Never had it washed off.
    Yet with all the more love
        I went unto you
And you prospered into a kingdom.

III
I must go away to abroad.
    When I returned uptown
I met you and you knew me not,
    Your hair like flax tow   40

Crimped like an eggbeater, your
Mouth like a cannibal's—bloody,
Your eyelids massive with blue mud,
    A handmuff of bats fur.

I found out your carryings on,
    Your lovers and infidelities.
You sold my child to a brothel,
    You had to pay for your men.

In pity, I bribed men to go to you,
    To your two biggest lovers,   50
        Lord Dragon and Count Ceros,
I whispered your infamies.

They gathered their mobs of devils,
In the name of virtue they attacked
        Your tall town house
As you bore a seven month bastard.

Out on your balcony they brought you,
    Your house devoured with fire.
Out they threw you and the dogs
    Licked your blood up.   60

IV
    Then from your hand I took
My ring, from the witch's hand
    I took my golden ring.
    Her breast was a dungheap.

    Her child I found and I
    Washed you in my tears.
Still on your shoulder is the
    Red speck that I know.

I wash you with my tears
    And still the speck remains.   70
It is my fault, my darling,
    That I have not tears enough.

1959

Granny Crack

I was a leather skinned harridan
I wandered the county's roads
Trading and begging and fighting
With the sun for hat and the road for shoes.

You played a pigsty Venus
When you were young, old dame,
In the graveyard or behind the tavern.
The burdock girl was your name.

She talked vilely it is remembered,
Was a moving and walking dictionary   10
Of slang and unconventional language
The detail of her insults was extraordinary.

We dozen scoundrels laid you
For a quarter each in the ditch
To each you gave the sensation
That we were the exploited bitch.

You saw me freckled and spotted
My face like a killdeer's egg
When, berry-picking kids, you ran from me
Frightened down the lane by the wood.   20

They saw her as an incredible crone
The spirit of neglected fence corners,
Of the curious wisdom of brambles
And weeds, of ruts, of stumps and of things despised.

I was the mother of your sun
I was the sister of your moon
My veins are your paths and roads
On my head I bear steeples and turrets
I am the darling of your god.

1959

The Ghost

The evening waddles over the fields like a turkey.
I lurk,
Where my knowledge was chopped from my power.
All knowledge waits for you at the corner here so murky.

The awkward doltish low I.Q. farmboy shambles down the steps,
The empty echoing pitcher in his hand:
I am!
Ha ha! And his hair stands straight up like brambles.

Everything — Egyptian hieroglyphs and crystallography,
Diary of shadows,   10
Vast God and the interiors of tree trunks, snowflakes
All spin like a fiery corkscrew into his psychology.

For I know everything now having passed into source,
Even
Through me he knows himself — a kidnapped prince.
It is too much for him — he falls down — hoarse
As they shriek and lift him up — I am not.

The evening waddles over the fields like a turkey.
I lurk,
Where my knowledge was severed from my power.   20
All knowledge waits for you at the corner here so murky.

1959

A SEQUENCE IN FOUR KEYS

i) The Dwarf

Six inches of my six foot pa
Compressed my height to these three feet.
On Sabbath day he sold me to
The castle of the starry street

There I sleep in a cradle and amuse
The castle with my minority.
No, I am not someone far away.
Reach out and touch me.

I plucked a berry for the young queen
Such fruit as drove her mad.   10
She haunts the stables and the mews,
Is serviced by the coachman's lad.

I stole the tall crown prince's toy
And put it in his brother's chest.
He knocked his brother out of life
With father's curse he fled to east.

The servants swore that they saw angels;
I said that they must grovel,
I sneered and laughed at all their visions.
Now they see only hovel.   20

The swineherd was a noble man,
More noble than my lord.
With a whicker-whack I tripped him up.
His brow now levels swineward.

'Twas I who hid beneath the bed
When the princess planned elopement.
They got as far as the Scarlet Sea
When my lord's riders they met.

I filled their hearts with maddening lust,
I made three eyes unfashionable,   30
I filled their hearts with maddening chastity,
I split them into sexual.

Lady Air and Sir Earth,
Alderman Water and the Earl of Fire,
Yeoman Quintessence and Miss Light
I set at jar and gyre and ire.

123

From this casement look ye out
At rotting sheep and mildewed crop.
There's the minstrel limping off
I bade them yesterday his tongue lop.   *40*

The castle's empty, wonder none —
I bade them re-build it inside out.
Their fire flew up into the sun,
Their cistern rolled into a moon.

In a great battle my dear lord
Killed and was killed by the crown prince.
I've holed up here among the ruins
The compressed cause of everything.

The only thing I know how to do
Is crawl into this manger.   *50*
I'll prop the dead queen's body up,
Perhaps 'twill fool a stranger.

Come here shepherds.   Here's the way.
Bah bah bah for an incarnation.
This way aristocratic intelligence.
Meow meow for a new sensation!

To the curious observant baby
The humble and the royal bow.
Hush a bye my baby do, for see —
The spider on your mother's brow.   *60*

ii) The Baby

Small babe, tell me
        As you sat in your mother's cave
What did you build there,
        Little baby mine?

Sir, I made the tooth
        I invented the eye
I played out hair on a comb-harp
        I thought up the sigh.

I pounded the darkness to
        Guts, Heart and Head: *10*
America, Eurasia and Africa
        I out of chaos led.

124

I fought the goblins
        For the heart;
'Twas a jewel they desired,
        But I held it.

I fought off the rats
        From the guts
They nibbled but I
        Smashed the mutts.   20

I choked the bat so intent
        For the diamond of my mind;
I caught him in the ogre's cellar
        The tub of blood behind.

And the darkness gave me
        Two boneless wands or swords;
I knew not their meaning then
        Whether traps or rewards.

One was the vorpal phallus
        Filled with jostling army,   30
Henhouse and palace
        Street crowds and history.

Two was the magic tongue
        Stuffed with names and numbers,
The string of song
        The waker from fallen slumbers.

My mother opened her grave
        I sprang out a giant
Into another cave
        Where I was a seed again,   40

Helpless and wriggly small
        As in my father's groin;
My Shakespeare's tongue a wawl
        And impotent my loin.

The sun-egg I must reach
        Was steeples far away,
The world that I must name
        Was shapeless, sneaky gray.

Is it wonder then I rage
        An old man one hour old,   50
A bridegroom come to a bride
        Careless unready and cold.

My wedding cake's still in the field;
    My bride is ninety and maggotty;
My groomsmen glaring hangmen;
    My bridal bed bouldery.

Small babe, tell me
    As you sit in your mother's cave
What do you build there,
    Little baby mine?   60

iii) The Dauphin

The emperor has a dart for eye,
    The household guards fight on,
The Patriarch waits at His door,
    The world we know is at an end.

The golden nightingale will pass
    Into uncircumcized mint;
A thousand grubby hands will grasp
    And clip, and bank and profit.

Tons of night lie on the heart;
    The darkness wallows, deepens and slides   10
In ponderous clouds of doom
    Through which the ancient nurse glides.

Through the storm of fear, against
    The wind of dread, through the sea
Of blood, along the wall and across
    Into the forest of a time to be.

The burning city and the exultant foe
    Thunder their victory:
From the charcoal burner's hut
    Comes the answering cry.   20

"It shall not be your evil cross
    Will long have this power.
When I grow up I the King shall come
    And stand in my tower."

As the Sultan swung the Patriarch's head
    Like a lantern by the beard
He heard a distant infant's cry
    The fearfullest sound he ever heard.

It was the cry that Herod heard
      From the young lion in Bethlehem   *30*
It is the cry that the dark sea hates
      The cry of the source.

The man is the child of a child
      The dark sea's the child of the rain
In the forest there sleeps the young seed
      The king who will come again.

iv) The Lost Child

Long have I looked for my lost child.
I hear him shake his rattle
Slyly in the winter wind
In the ditch that's filled with snow.

He pinched and shrieked and ran away
At the edge of the November forest.
The hungry old burdock stood
By the dead dry ferns.

Hear him thud that ball!
The acorns fall by the fence.   *10*
See him loll in the St. Lucy sun,
The abandoned sheaf in the wire.

Oh Life in Death! my bonny nursling
Merry drummer in the nut brown coffin,
With vast wings outspread I float
Looking and looking over the empty sea

And there! in the — on the rolling death
Rattling a dried out gourd
Floated the mysterious cradle
Filled with a source.   *20*

I push the shore and kingdom to you,
Oh winter walk with seedpod ditch:
I touch them to the floating child
And lo! Cities and gardens, shepherds and smiths.

1959

The City

Old London/New London

Blow the trumpet! Beat the drum!
We've come to a happy place.
For here is old London town
And we'll stay here a space.

The river & tide lead on our ship.
On those flat lands live smugglers
And salesmen of drowned men's clothes.
Ah! thirty & two swans.

Ho ho over there you hanged pirate!
You're a bony tattered flag!   10
Hush! There's the castle,
The knot that ties up the whole bag.

Hark! the innocent priest is shrieking.
Lo! the imprisoned poet's sighing.
Hear the unransomed dauphin crying.
Hear the spy scream: "You're lying!"

Well, we'll alight at this ancient wharf,
Just ahead is the ancient bridge.
Our sailors know their taverns & whores
But we're for a completer voyage.   20

This is the criminal quarter.
Hear them squeaking in their sleep.
All the laws in the law books
Find a breaker in this heap.

Look at those kids-- gutter rolling pins.
My God, what are they doing!
Of course, they learn that early.
Hear that baby boohooing.

Here is the lawyer's college
Where the children of the prosperous   30
Learn the laws to trap the criminals
And put them in the jail house.

What was that gurgly plop
As we stepped upon the bridge?
Oh you know these merchants rupt.
The suicide floats in the sludge.

Now here are the wooden cupids!
These are the houses called stews.
Violets and Pansies running with pus,
The bishop has licensed their hues.   40

Let us look in at the archbishop
In his palace of holy hardware.
His dilemma is that he has power
And yet must translate its destroyer.

"Ferryman! We want across!" Tell me
Why it– what keeps it all going?
The answer is that in your hand
Stamped with the face of the king.

This metal flat cake *is* the king,
His nobles & his parliament.   50
Misers put it through their bowels
To clean the tarnish off it.

What are those shrieks from that building?
A woman is bearing a child?
Oh I could smash that clock!
Hear its woodpecker ticking bell.

Why here are some people laughing
At the entrance to a kirk,
A bride & a proper young bridegroom
Advance through the graveyard murk.   60

But what's that black bear
Eating up those chimneys,
A black bear forty feet high
With shrill stars for eyes?

My friend, that was a funeral.
Here's the hospital for the insane.
The city's got into their heads, poor things,
How'd you like a street for a brain?

The light comes in at the windows,
The dark goes down to the cellar.   70
But the dark now comes up from the cellar
A spider with one vast leg.

But you've thrown away your genitals,
Chopped off your hands & feet,
Knocked off your head like a pumpkin.
My friend, I don't call this sweet.

Goodbye, my ancient tower
And great big church on the hill.
Our ship floats out on the tide
Two & thirty swans until.   80

Dear sweet swans who resemble
The two and thirty teeth
Of a city monster that we've built
To crouch on the world's wild heath.

1959

The Man Hunter

After the flare of the illegal action
"A Mr. Ledger was found murdered"
Society assembles me, fills my heart
With blood, my brain with purpose and my

I walk through the arranged spaces
Plain clothes over my iron flesh:
I go to alleys, lanes, squares & places,
I tip the beer parlour this way & that.

I pull the transom to me
And walk through baby's minds   10
I climb through the children's game
And negotiate the hopscotch rinds.

Bye bye Baby Bunting
Daddy's gone a-hunting
Gone to get a criminal's skin
To wrap my Baby Bunting in.

I am caught in the old woman's hair;
That pumpkin she calls her head
Cannot remember; the brick leaves flutter,
The steel trees and the cement underwood.   20

I have reached the turn in the path,
The ford through the fountains of traffic,
I hang on a saliva rope from the tramp's
Cliff-face—it is the last mountain.

The pawn ticket: Mr. Ledger's obscene music box.
Existence fastens its minute teeth in my
The advertising hits with its whore-sonnets
The street car crawls up my thigh

The chestnut leaves play card games,
The street lights each have a separate system of shadows,   30
I come to my Sleeping Beauty, my New Jerusalem,
The man with the words on his forehead: FORGIVE ME

Front Street and Duke Street and Jarvis
I married my hempen princess
Timothy Eaton Memorial United Church
I put a human neck in her circle.

1959

131

A MESSAGE TO WINNIPEG

Speaker:
Inside the city where noone listened to the poet made up
of one thousand rice paper Bible pages the people lived
on the streets that had names and walked up and rode
down these same streets that had names except of course
the Indians who lived in Roosterville and the tramps
who lived in old packing cases by the river and the
hermit who lived in the centre of the ancient dump in an
old old old car which he had sodded over so that it was
a car made out of earth and grass with only one wheel—
the earth, our world, itself.   10

i) The Factory

Where the railways suddenly twist
    By the central drainage ditch
Across an unused waste of ground
    Stands this huge palace.

A severe stern-eyed tall object,
    The great house of an efficient king,
    Hundreds of eyes yet unadorned,
    Informal gardens of sowthistling.

Inside huge wheels spin and belts Ixion,
    Eight hundred workers swarm   20
    Lifting ritual corkscrews, snipping,
    Cutting the sacred pattern.

There was no king here, no scullion either,
    Pretty well all the same:
Old Bill Field hit the same nail
    For fifty years of star-flame.

It wasn't majestic, it wasn't squalid.
    It might have been more exciting.
As a matter of fact it was horrible!
    But it can't quite be put down in writing.   30

The icicles glittered from the windowsills
The summer storms lashed the eyed cliff:
    A huge force lived there!
A giant prince mysteriously stiff.

The thing is he's not enchanted
    As a matter of fact he's free
    Enslaved by his own freedom.

132

How's that for a quest, my dear listener;
  I'll call you—St. Georgy-Porgy.

Speaker:
I walk down the street conscious that this has   40
not always been like this.
I walk down the street knowing that this has not
always been so.
Once there could have been a burial mound instead
of the factory.

ii) *Winnipeg Seen as a Body of Time and Space*

Winnipeg, what once were you. You were,
Your hair was grass by the river ten feet tall,
Your arms were burr oaks and ash leaf maples,
Your backbone was a crooked silver muddy river,
Your thoughts were ravens in flocks, your bones were   50
        snow,
Your legs were trails and your blood was a people
        Who did what the stars did and the sun.

Then what were you? You were cracked enamel like
Into parishes and strips that come down to the river.
Convents were built, the river lined with nuns
Praying and windmills turning and your people
Had a blood that did what a star did and a Son.

Then on top of you fell
A boneyard wrecked auto gent, his hair
Made of rusted car door handles, his fingernails   60
Of red Snowflake Pastry signs, his belly
Of buildings downtown; his arms of sewers,
His nerves electric wires, his mouth a telephone,
His backbone—a cracked cement street. His heart
An orange pendulum bus crawling with the human fleas
Of a so-so civilization—half gadget, half flesh—
    I don't know what I would have instead—
    And they did what they did more or less.

Speaker:
In the past it was decided. While the English beat
the French at Waterloo the French Métis beat the   70
English at the Battle of Seven Oaks but then in the
end, dear listener, Waterloo counted for more than
Seven Oaks.

133

iii) Le Tombeau de Pierre Falcon

Pierre Falcon,
You say here along with this unsingable music
That on June nineteenth these Burnt Wood people
Ah yes, the Métis were dark, so called Bois-Brûlés,
Arrived near this settlement of Lord Selkirk's
Fort Douglas

You say in this second verse that your Burnt Woods
Took three foreigners prisoner at Frog Plain.   *80*
These foreigners were Scotchmen from the Orkneys
Who had come, as you put it, to rob your—Pierre
    Falcon's—
Country.

Well we were just about to unhorse
When we heard two of us give, give voice.
Two of our men cried, "Hey! Look back, look back!
    The Anglo-Sack
    Coming for to attack."

Right away smartly we veered about
Galloping at them with a shout!   *90*
You know we did trap all, all those Grenadiers!
    They could not move
    Those horseless cavaliers.

Now we like honourable men did act,
Sent an ambassador—yes, in fact!
"Monsieur Governor! Would you like to stay?
    A moment spare—
    There's something we'd like to say."

Governor, Governor, full of ire.
"Soldiers!" he cries, "Fire! Fire."   *100*
So they fire the first and their muskets roar!
    They almost kill
    Our ambassador!

Governor thought himself a king.
He wished an iron rod to swing.
Like a lofty lord he tries to act.
    Bad luck, old chap!
    A bit too hard you whacked!

When we went galloping, galloping by
Governor thought that he would try   110
For to chase and frighten us Bois-Brûlés.
     Catastrophe!
     Dead on the ground he lay.

Dead on the ground lots of grenadiers too.
Plenty of grenadiers, a whole slew.
We've almost stamped out his whole army.
     Of so many
     Five or four left there be.

You should have seen those Englishmen—
Bois-Brûlés chasing them, chasing them.   120
From bluff to bluff they stumbled that day
     While the Bois-Brûlés
     Shouted "Hurray!"

And now in this eleventh verse you ask
Who made up this song and then you tell us
That you yourself made it up—Pierre Falcon.
You made it up to sing the glory of the
Burnt Wood People.

Far away and dear, spunky old and early poet
I wish I could sing the praises of the Neon People   130
To You.

Speaker:
I walked through the streets of Winnipeg
The ice glittered on the gargoyles and statues
High up on the 1913 boom business buildings
I thought of Pierre Falcon and I thought of

iv) Traffic

Red Orange Green Arrows Side Streets No Parking,
A car with a headache, it looks like a shark,
Glittering, really rather beautiful; demonic engine
Humming to the children and the old ladies—Come
     here,
Under my wheels and I'll toss you. Glittering   140
Hard merciless cars. Glittering hard merciless
Cars. Extremely useful, extremely depressing
Who would have thought that this
Was the freedom they fought for.

135

The translator of the Bible who ended up at the stake
Wrote with his pen this corner mashed with autos
Waiting to go, waiting to be stopped.
Everyone their own coach and horses
Everyone their own control of space.
Of course the problem of how to get there is solved—   150
But what gets there? What gets there is what gets there.
Red Orange Green Arrows Side Streets No Parking,
A Car with a headache, it looks like a shark.

Speaker:
If you should walk down Portage Avenue
If you should walk down Portage Avenue
If you should walk down Portage Avenue

v) A Crowd

Walk, Don't Walk, Run for your Life, Green, Red,
    Purple
  Roar, Hum
Miss Handlebar and Mr. Steering Wheel, Master
    Accelerator
Were in the crowd as well as all these others   160
  In between Eaton's and the Bay
Mr. and Mrs. Pushbutton, Mr. and Mrs. Eggbeater and
Little Miss Weasel, Mr. Mould, Mr. Coffin, Miss Casket,
Mr. Embalmer, Mr. Funeral Home, Miss Undertook,
Master Window, Mr. Box, Old Mrs. Cocoanut, Granny
    Plague,
Miss Light, Mr. Short, Miss Belly, Young Cigarette, Old
    Bum
Mr. Dim Radio, Miss Ghastly Hollow, the Lieutenant
    Governor,
Television Mouth, a dwarf, Miss Idiot, Professor
    Twaddle,
Doctor Horror, Assistant Professor Sulky, and Mother
    Neurosis
Some Hutterites with geese under their arms, Father   170
    Monster,
And the Sliver girls: Little Sliver, Just as little Sliver,
    Sliver,
Old Spit, Young Kleenex and twenty-five Albanians
  Were in the crowd as well as all these others
    In between Eaton's and the Bay.

Speaker:
When I first came to this city I lived in a boarding
house, there were still street cars, a friend of mine
taught me to play chess, the chess champion for
Canada lives here, this is a way you could see the
city and once upon a time I would have closed the
sequence with this poem.   180

vi) *Winnipeg as a Chess Game*

It is a game of chess or checkers.
No, it is a game of chess
For we have not all the same
Income, outcome, stations, riches.
It is a game of civilization
Played on squares of Night and Day.
A life in a city, a life in playing
Games of getting up and going to bed,
Being alive and being so dead,
How to be good and how to be bad   190
Upon the squares of summer,
In the corner of spring
With the children skipping,
In the white streets of winter
Beneath the brown leaves with trees on them
In the fall park.

I went
Down the streets where I have seen
In an upstairs room, the White Queen,
With a bicycle beside her bed.   200
I looked
In a window on York Street,
Saw the White Knight and three pawns
All round a table eating their supper.
I had not had mine yet and loved
The match girl orphan loneliness
Of watching other people eating theirs:
Passing the saltshaker, reaching for the butter.
The rest of the white pawns rushed through the street,
Playing games of frontier and boycows and buffalogirls;   210
They skipped with pieces of string coming
With secretive paper bags out of the Gem Store.

Everytime I go out I bring back
A face I love, a face I didn't notice,
I bring back another black piece,
Another white one for the game.
I met the black pieces on Donald Street.
Beside the funeral home I saw a yellow car.
Then in the night they come toward me
Dark, dark faces, negroes in ones and twos   220
Going towards the funeral of their black king,
King of the black people in a city of snow.

Down this street I went and saw
A small girl shooting with a bow and arrow.
Her father's house was a house where
Hands and cups were read and she
Was a pawn in the centre of the board.

Down the street the streetcar comes
And while it comes you cannot talk   230
Until you board it, the old streetcar
Young once in Philadelphia sixty years ago they say,
Long room with a stove, company,
Strangers and green moss to sit upon.
As we move to see the Black Queen,
The White Bishop, old Canon Bastion,
Is on the car with us and says Hello.
He never understands but has a voice
Fit for anything in the King James Version

We go to see the Black Queen   240

Each day after Christmas the sun sets farther north
Of Broadway

All these white streets of winter
Filled with walking people
This castle turns a corner
This woman takes a pawn
Reader I present you with a chessboard in the snow

Speaker:
But I do not feel like that anymore.
Or, at any rate, it is a submerged feeling.
Winnipeg is a loutish giant sucking a sugar beet beside   250
            the two winding rivers.

Winnipeg you are a city the same as the London of the
          Empire that spawned you, the Athens and Rome
          that still
transmit some of their patterns to you sitting in the
          swamp
at the forks of the river You are like Babylon and like
Nineveh You are any city and there is one thing you
must be told:

Over the plain and under the sky
  The signposts whirl like weathervanes.   260
The sun guesses where his shadow to throw,
  The four hooves crash the puddle ice panes

He draws the mountain to him,
  He fattens the distant speck,
Away! I've no time for you, he says;
  He scampers the lake and the beck.

The forest he shovels past,
  Dark branch cannot hold him,
The geese expand in the village
  The chimneys and steeples brim: 270

He says—in the market place
  To windows and faces and crowns
Eyes and keyholes and dogs
  Sides and tops, ups and downs—

Leave the burning city
  Leave this burning town
Destruction cometh — a sucking cloud,
  Your towers will tumble down

Child's Restaurant will be consumed
  Eaton's and Hudson's Bay   280
Grass will grow on your neon signs
  And the rivers dry away

But this city is not burning,
  A wise old idiot says,
And there's no war we've heard of:
The young matrons titter and gaze.

The messenger beats his brow
  The stupid pavement ups,
The ignorant buildings close him in,
  The street plan him cups.   290

Till Winnipeg Babylon becomes him,
  The city disappears,
And over the plain and under the sky
  He gallops with truthful fear.

Leave this burning city!
  Will noone listen me?
Even now the doomfist knocks!
It's the sound of our hearts, say we.

Over the plain and under the sky
Over the plain and under the sky   300
Over the plain and under the sky
Over the plain and under the sky

1960

4

A SUIT
OF NETTLES –
1958

A
GOOSE: *Welsh*, gwyz; *Danish*, gaas; *Saxon*, gos; *Russian*, gus; *Latin*, anser; *Greek*, Χήν; *Sanskrit*, hansá; *Italian*, oca; *German*, die Gans; *French*, l'oie; *Spanish*, ganso; a general name for the large web-footed birds of the subfamily Anserinae, usually larger than a duck, and smaller than a swan.

B
Old Mother Goose,
When she wanted to wander,
Would ride through the air
On a very fine gander.

C
Gray goose and gander,
   Waft your wings together,
And carry the good king's daughter
   Over the one-strand river.

D
Goosey Goosey Gander where shall we wander . . .

E
The devil damn thee black, thou cream-faced loon!
Where gott'st thou that goose look?
            Macbeth

F
Let there be gall enough in thy ink, though thou write with a goose-pen, no matter.
            Twelfth Night

G
Now tall Agrippa lived close by—
So tall, he almost touch'd the sky;
He had a mighty inkstand, too,
In which a great goose-feather grew.
            Struwwelpeter

H

What a goose you are. In the Egyptian hieroglyphics the emblem of a vain silly fellow is a goose.

I

The coat of arms of the Company of Musicians—viz., a swan, with expanded wings, within a double tressure (the gridiron), counter, flory, argent. Perverted into a goose striking the bars of a gridiron with its foot, and called 'The Swan and Harp,' or 'Goose and Gridiron.'

J

In the times of popery here were no less than eighteen houses on the Bankside, licensed by the Bishops of Winchester . . . to keep whores, who were, therefore, commonly called Winchester Geese.

K

For good society is but a game, 'The royal game of Goose,' as I may say.
        Byron

L

Galen might goe shooe the Gander for any good he could doo. . . .
        Nashe

M

Christmas is a-comin' and the geese are getting fat.

N & ETC.

I wish, gentlemen, it was one of the geese of Ferrara, so much celebrated among the ancients for the magnitude of their livers, one of which is said to have weighed upwards of two pounds. With this food, exquisite as it was, did Heliogabulus regale his hounds.
        Smollett

To the Reader

This poem was written out of interest in a number of things: geese, country life in Ontario, Canada as an object of conversation and Edmund Spenser's *Shepherd's Calendar*. The *Shepherd's Calendar*, published in 1579, is a collection of dialogues between shepherds named Hobbinoll, Colin, Cuddie, Piers, Thomalin, Morrell, Thenot and so on. Since there is a dialogue for each month we are able to watch a complete English year pass before our eyes with its variety of weathers, crops and animals. Hobbinoll wishes to be Colin's friend; Colin loves Rosalind for the entire calendar without any encouragement. At the end of the poem she has gone off with someone else. Cuddie is rather saucy to an old shepherd, Thenot, who reproves him with a fable about the Oak and the Briar. Willie and Thomalin discuss Cupid who has shot Thomalin in the heel and was once captured by Willie's father in a fowler's net. Piers and Palinode argue about Protestant and Catholic shepherds—which are the better. In August Willie and Perigot put on a singing match judged by Cuddie and so on. There are plaintive love-sick eclogues caused by Colin's miserable love affair, merry careless eclogues when the shepherds dance or sing and dark bitter eclogues when the sad state of the church and the poet are reviewed.

In *A Suit of Nettles* readers will notice that there are dialogues between geese named Mopsus, Branwell, Effie, Dorcas, Raymond, Duncan, Fanny and others. Branwell is the slightly ridiculous figure of melancholy itself wrapped up in a suit of nettles he has put on in order to emphasize his sorrow at a fair goose's inattention. The reader will find fables, sestinas, singing matches, the passage of a year in the Ontario countryside—many of the things already mentioned as being in the *Shepherd's Calendar*. The Church satirized in A *Suit of Nettles* is that defined by Coleridge as comprising all the intellectual institutions of the age. These institutions sometimes nourish the educational theory and the literary criticism condemned in *July* and *August*, and the mental attitude described in *May*. Scrutumnus stands for *Scrutiny*, the famous critical quarterly edited by Dr F.R. Leavis which ceased to be published some years ago. *May* arises from an incident reported in *Life* concerning some fanatics in the populous Kentucky mountains. *July* springs from a fabulous CBC *Citizens' Forum* in which Dr Hilda Neatby trounced a progressive educational theorist. The system of education suggested by Valancy's remarks resembles that of the ancient Irish bards. In the long note 'appended' to *August*, for 'God's Universe' and 'God's Tiger' read *Finnegans Wake* and Blake's *Tiger*, both victims of evaluation. In *September*, Bishop Bourget is the Pouter Pigeon, his victim is Guibord. Creighton's history of Canada, *Dominion of the North*, gives you the facts, as well as the background for 'Dante's Inferno,' an attempt to compress Canadian history and geography into a single horrific scenic railway ride. Some of the things said about glaciers and their products have their source in a book of D.J. Putnam called *The Physiography of Southern Ontario*. By the way, 'Mome Fair' is a careful imitation of the annual Fall Fair held in many small Ontario towns; the prize animals, birds and flowers as well as the carnival rides. Last of all, in Ontario there are, as I count them, forty-three counties, the forty-three fields mentioned in the second eclogue.

145

Invocation to the Muse of Satire

With Punch's stick (he holds it in his hand)
Beat fertility into a sterile land,
With hands of hawthorn branches in the winter,
And teeth of cold March rain that bite the soft snow,
And bristly porcupines on which the hunter sits for hair;
With skin of mildew and botfly holes poked through
In hide of long impounded, ancient cow,
With eyes whose tears have quotaed out to ice long ago,
Eyes bright as the critical light upon the white snow;
With arms of gallows wood beneath the bark   10
And torso made of a million hooked unhooking things,
And legs of stainless steel, knives & scythes bunched together,
And feet with harrows, and with discs for shoes—
Speak, Muse of Satire, to this broken pen
And from its blots and dribbling letter-strings
Unloose upon our farm & barnyard—medicine.

With those feet, dance upon their toes
With those legs, grasp them lovingly about the thighs
With that torso, press against their breasts
With those arms, hug them black and blue   20
With those eyes, look at them you love
With that cheek, rub against their cheeks
With that hair, put your head down in their laps
With those teeth, give forth playful bites
And shake their hands with hour-long explorations
Of their life and heart and mind-line,
But with that stick of which new ones spring ever
From that vine where it was barbarously cut off,
Beat them about the ears and the four senses
Until, like criminals lashed in famine time,   30
They bring forth something; until thy goad
Grows so warm it bursts into blossoms.

Here, lady, almost blind with seeing too much
Here is the land with spires and chimneys prickly,
Here is the east of the board and here the west,
Here may you enter and there, before you depart,
May you make the sky red with doom and axey wrath.

Has no one seen the country where your cure has nursed?
It is a land of upturned privies with occupants inside them
Crawling out through new tops like astonished moths   40
Bursting from their unusual, foul and dark cocoons.

146

JANUARY

Argument

*In this first eclogue two geese, Branwell & Mopsus, discuss the different
kinds of love. Branwell is wearing a suit made out of nettles.*

With the other geese within the goosehouse
There lived, I know not how, various kinds
Of geese: some like a cat, some like a mouse,
Some like a groundhog and some like lions,
Some like two straight parallel lines,
Others more circular in character,
Some shallow and some deep as mines,
Others than chaos far more muddier,
And whether you should parcel fast or loose
Some could not be but simply described 'Goose.'   10

      Branwell   Mopsus

You there, old Mopsus, you're no bird.
I see distinctly limbs beneath the feathers;
You've got a voice too that was never heard
Just in springtime, but in all the weathers.
Do not stand agog at these green tatters;
Crossed in love I'll wear them till my death.
Mopsus, is there purpose in the pulse one gathers
Wristful by wristful? Mopsus, spend thy breath
In talking as I hear you can of geese
And life and whether they and all and life should cease.   20

Mopsus
It might! And no time's better than this month,
The two-faced time whose sun no more goes south,
And in its cold there comes a milk white moth
Of frozen breath from horse and warm cow mouth
As they run down to pond to cure their drouth;
Old Brown's crowbar breaks the ice beforehand
To give new life to their lives so uncouth,
But need not do so if you understand:
By next September we could stop all life—
Let no one break the ice, let no man take a wife.   30

Branwell
But should we smother all creation outright?

Mopsus
Here stands a woman with attractive dugs
And here a dugless wise old anchorite;
She leads a life of grotesque scarecrow hugs,
His eyes slide over Bibles slow as slugs;
She tempts you down a well of luscious shame

147

That into world another funeral lugs,
Another longing for the whence it came,
More jumping in and out of needles' eyes,
More love poems, paradoxes, happy unions, lies.   40

From some old grim geneva-gowned bore
Proto-orthodox, the hermit lifts his eyes
And gelds you from the world with sermons frore
About the cleansing of the foul heart's sties
With fasts, with baking private humble pies,
Feeling fear, dread, repentance, god-desire,
God-terror, god-damnation till you rise
Downwards from your knees to worlds of dire
Pathless woods of rungless Jacob's ladders
Set in hollows filled with aspen-voiced adders.   50

But do not follow either of these devils,
Reject Elijah—swear off Jezebel,
Come to my ferny groves by calm canals
Where all is bland correct and rational;
Our friendship we'll develop cell by cell,
Investigating what one can't believe;
Attached to all that is unphysical
We'll talk and muse until we must take leave.
Some call that death, but our minds meshed together
Will note the new unbodied time as but a change in weather.   60

Here look at man. I'll draw him in this dung.
Here the arms like shrivelled legs that uphoist
Spoons of outside world for wet mouth-tongue.
Beneath here hear his bellows groan and hiss:
Dreary East Wind sucked in bladder moist,
Expelled in warm coughs, shrieks, words, cries, alarums:
This knot hides stomach's greedy frog-jump cess,
These legs look like great dropsy ogre arms,
Here Love has chosen Sewer for his mate,
You'd marry this, you'd copy this, you'd propagate!   70

Climb up with me into this peastraw loft
Where rustlings strange this afternoon have come.
Above the geese Ann and the hired boy coughed,
Their bodies adding up the lovers' sum.
What oneness is there now to this relation?
Their joined mouths comprise a sort of union,
His teeth against her teeth with skull tension.
So with a short leap now his passions come.
Look how she breathes him in and out thro' snout
Of Hell, and so were we from Heaven tumbled out!   80

I do not think he loves her nor she him;
They love the deed, but not I think each other.
You say you love through girl her elohim,

You love her soul and not your selfish pleasure,
But how be sure? With me your steadfast brother
Be certain of the soul's affection; never
Could we stoop to this foul mad disorder.
Come Light, Fire and Sun from planets sever,
Possess the Love and Light that does not use
This stake and heart-of-vampire sexual eye of ooze.   90

Branwell
But is this light, my dear friend Mopso,
That never falls on darkness but between
The nine sick planets would to nothing go?
Can I desire one whit of world I've seen
Displayed in your cartography of spleen?
I shiver at its top, that round cold sea.
Without some isle a sea's a dismal scene.
The world's hot middle where it's he and she
Has grown for me feverish stinging clothes.
Your favourite land is better I agree—   100
What a round concrete continent of snows!
But too round and too continent for me
For I want offspring summerson autumnman wintersage
And tricklerrain thawwind panetap upleaf windrage
Plow and seed and hoe, green, sucklepig, yellowripe,
sicklestraw and all such glamourie.

FEBRUARY

Argument

*Branwell's fiancée, Dorcas, has returned from a stay at the farmhouse:
it turns out that she has double-crossed Branwell again and there is a
big fight among the geese in the goosehouse.*

The sun begets, the moon bears, tides away
Rush into coastal caves: 'Men do bear not'
[*The Courtier*] 'their children for a day,'
But women longer, for a nine moon trot;
The young cub forms like a dim loose star-knot
In the lioness as down the sun sets,
Night wobbles in, and spirit goslings sought
To dance this month through the small small eyelets
Of birth before birth, death before death pinned
Resolved & tight in each large goose egg's centre inned.   10

'Occurocceroo,' crowed Thompson the cock,
His small throat tied fast to the giant sun
Kicking aside the night as it rose: 'Bock!
Giddibock giddibock!' cried then each one
Of those who gave Dorcas Goose a welcome.
A pretty girl was Dorcas, a pet goose;

Back in the gooseshed was she after some
Time with a broken leg up at the house;
In the best corner sat she with her glass
Primping & being admired by all geese *en masse.*   20

> *Effie   Dorcas   Branwell   Mopsus*

Where did you get that button & string
You wear so prettily around your neck?

Dorcas
My mistress gave me this pretty dear thing,
She loved me much, so did me pretty deck.
She gave me also corn & pease to peck,
And I learnt all the secrets of their place
When by my basket underneath Quebec*
The cat & dog talked all my mind could trace:
Cellar, pantry, woodshed, upstairs, downstairs!
O strange words that beat a goose's wildest nightmares!   30

Now these new things of which you've never heard
Let me explain; first the cellar where they
Keep preserves and roots and cream and white curd,
Butter and cheese, pitchers of milk and whey.
Close to each other, but not too, they lay
Apples, red brown and yellow in their bins,
And all in shadows deep dark down from day
Rows of cider barrels huge as dead kings,
Beside a cistern where a trapped cloud lies
Beside the air where Scug the bat scallops and flies.   40

He hangs from beam in winter upside down
But in the spring he right side up lets go
And flutters here and there zigzagly flown
Till up the chimney of the house quick-slow
He pendulum-spirals out in light low
Of sunset swinging out above the lawns
Gathering sinking insects' sag downflow
Returning as the light on green world dawns
And down the chimney disappears nimble
To the cellar where they catch mice with a thimble.   50

Catch them with cheese in thimble poised 'neath bowl.
This lizard-haunt bears other rooms above
Where stoves are warm when outside cold winds howl—
The pantry, dining room, the parlour clove
Apart with hallway and the kitchen move
Around me thinking of that dear gold time.
How oft, my mistress softer than a dove

---

* Dorcas means a Quebec stove; unless she means she was in Ontario
which is under Quebec on a map.

Their piano bade me to play and climb
To watch the eight-day clock from their table;
Better far than sun to keep time it is able.   60

Old wallpapers beneath the wallpaper
Buried throughout the years in all the rooms
Over plaster, over logs their father,
Grandfather knocked clear out of wilderdom's
Green thick-boled gnarled Indian-speckled glooms.
It's a guilty house, my girls; tho' we kill
Grass blades, they killed demon scores of green elms.
A dead savage lies beneath the door-sill,
The first son* played cards, went to proper-church;
The second son† did plot beneath a beer vat much.   70

There are some scratches still left on the floors
Where brothers fought, where distant relatives
Once stormed the place and roasted all the doors,
But since deaths of once-possessing natives
There's been no grand excitement save when lives
Of all the males were risked in thresh-machine:‡
Some came out alive, others half so; knives
And winnowers had quite threshed dead the others clean.
They chop down trees to build a gallows with;
Machines they build to thresh their gathered sons to death.   80

But the people living here are yet much
Like us: brick upon brick—they are new born,
They grow up, earn a living, learn prudence,
Depress a bed, beget a blockhead; mourn—
For the next brick seals them down, down, down, down.
And so this farmhouse stands upon the heels
Of forty-three large fields, their knot and crown.
Within, an ancient voice the silence steals:
Their heart beat, skull-hum, when it cries, are scarcely heard:
'Take us back to our beginning, white sail shipbird,   90

Uncut this forest old and our old countries green.'
Well girls, I now am ready for my beaus.
Pray step forward, gentlemen, and be seen.
Why by his weedy suit and burry hose
Here comes a suitor that one really knows.
Branwell it was come to welcome her back,
Long tortured with her melting shifty vows
His longing pushed him forth like a thumb tack;
He saw four buttons where was only one
So dizzed, so hoped he with a song to have her won.   100

---

* Family Compact   † Mackenzie   ‡ 1914

151

Branwell
My love I give to you a threefold thing,
A jewsharp serenade, a song I've made
And a sparkling pretty rose diamond ring.
To haste your love to me by fate delayed.
Zing zing zing zing, azeezing, azeezing,
Azuggazing, azeezug-zug-azing.

Six reasons are there for my loving you:
Your eyes, voice, beak, legs, mind and feathers white;
Feathers like snow, like cloud, like milk, like salt,
White white against the green grass in the spring.   110
Oh white angel in bethlehems of grime
Teach my slow wits to understand your worth.

With only reckless hope, not the true worth
That should raise up a suitor wooing you,
I try to know that stainless mind, so white
That crystal shafts and lily mines of salt
Seem when compared coal black: and in love's spring
I beg forgiveness for my own mind's grime.

Your paddling legs do even cleanse that grime;
When I scan all your parts and all your worth,   120
Sometimes they seem the prettiest part of you,
Those orange sticks beneath your body white,
Those sturdy swimming oars that somersault
Above your body at the pond in spring.

When your swift beak dives down for frog offspring,
Oh resting in his bathos hut of muddy grime
How sweet to be a frog that's nothing worth
Lifted to the sublime up up by you
By your fox orange beak and neck so white,
Your beak so bright it hurts the eye like salt.   130

Venison needs a humble pinch of salt;
You need the sounds that from your beak do spring,
Bragful when your feet feel spring's first thaw-grime,
Stout and most vigorous and strong when worth
We argue among us; rasping when you
See robbers in the yard with moonlight white.

But most I love—that's neither orange nor white—
Your circular blue eyes intense as salt:
They shot and caught my blizzardheart for spring,
First sky they cracked into my egg of grime,   140
First rain they let from out your storms of worth.
For these six things then I praise and love you
And now I beg you, my dread goddess white,
To slake my dry salt lips with mercy's spring
And touch my cold grime with your golden worth.

Dorcas
    Well, thank you very much but I am wed!
    Here, take your ring. Before I broke my leg
    In secrecy I married George.
                                    She laid,
    As all intook their breaths, a large white egg.   150
    It's George's child: the father shambles forth
A chop-the-harp and fish-with-the-strings sort of oaf.

    Branwell groaned. 'My ring!' cried his friend Mopsus
    'How could you give my gift to you to her,
    This gynerasty ruins its victims thus!
    Take that now you faithless thwarted changer!'
    Down to that dungy strawy chamber's floor
    Poor Branwell fell and got some kicks from George.
    Dorcas waddled up upon his form there
    And did the moral of it sweetly forge: 160

Dorcas
    Beneath me girls you see a dying swan;
Beside me view a goose: which race would you breed on?

Mopsus
    How dare you stand on top of my poor friend,
    Roared Mopsus charging from his corner sulk.
    He throttled Dorcas by her white wesand,
    He drove his beak full deep in George's bulk;
    George's stout friends then up did swiftly bulk:
    Now they were Zeke Gaspar Chauncey and Dob
    Hank and Hannibal, Grover and Quincy—
    A big muscular stout hot gander mob   170
    Ill temper flashing in their eyes like quinsy.
    Their wings flailed down on those of Mopsus' troop
Whose agile beaks enemy flesh and feather scoop.

    Nursing Dorcas as well as looking on,
    Her female friends now added to the noise.
    Their names were Trixy, Tilda, Jumping Joan,
    Letty, Etta, Moll, Pecunia, Eloise,
    Emma, Sadie as well as the two Zoes,
    One black handed, the other white handed.
    Their shrieks went up like rockets by small boys   180
    Sent up when school is burnt or disbanded.
    They bandaged George's wounded head and toe
But Mopsus' broken men they pummelled to and fro.

    Past the mash trough, bran tub and water pan
    Mopsus' allies were pressed sore hard at first;
    But soon past pan, past tub, past trough George ran
    Chased by Raymond a goose for blood athirst,
    A goose who longed to see George in a hearse.
    Three times he chased poor George round the mash trough,

153

Shouting vengeance on those who hated verse.   190
Just then to see what eggs she might take off
Ann came with pail; her boots were stuck with snow.
All battle ends as all to taste this latter go.

MARCH

Argument

*Branwell and Effie compare world pictures; his is understandably
rather gloomy. For good measure Effie recites a fable about the
doorknob and the door which argues for having some sort of handle to
your life whether you believe in it or not. Mopsus condescends to Effie
as if she were too bluestocking for him; actually from his speeches later
on you will see that Effie's attitude has had a great influence upon him.*

      Branwell   Effie   Mopsus

Lord, Lord, Effie, what fills you with such joy?
You are the drudge and scullion of this place
And yet you're lively as a wind-up toy.
You reach beneath each sitting goose with grace
And turn their eggs with pleasure on your face.
I'd puke at my hand being warmed that way;
I wince at how we reproduce our race.
How can you stand to do this night and day?
To midwife scores of cherubs into Hell
When you have reason to and can its horrors tell.   10

Did not your mother curse you as she died
After you'd changed her dressings for ten years;
Did she not often call you to her side
To twist your wing or box you on your ears?
Did she not fill all suitors' hearts with fears
That your womb could not nourish any seed?
She was to you what Dorcas was to me;
Love dreams, Love fails; Hate wakes and Hate succeeds,
For this is what rules fire earth air and sea—
A trapper with a trap of natural laws   20
That closes on all animals its starry jaws.

Effie
When we were small, Branwell, you thought not so.
We both then seemed to know of somewhere else
Than water earth and air and fire although
These things now seem all that is universe.
I dreamt I saw a white walled garden once
Where a child sat playing on a panpipe
Made, it seemed, of twinkling golden straw.
He stopped and asked me how I liked its shape;
I said its like for grace I never saw;

154

He said its straws were cut from a farm   *30*
In which our universe of stars is but a stone

   Sulking in fields of dew it cannot see.
   Branwell, I took my heart and opened it
   To better hear his strange glad minstrelsy.
   The shortest straw did to that dark place flit;
   Its everlasting music makes me fit
   To live through all ingratitude and dread,
   Rage, boredom and soul-starving deficit.
   If I prevent these eggs from being addled
   You must not sneer; this egg may hatch a heart   *40*
That will not close itself against a golden dart.

Branwell
   Well, I've a dream that strongly counters yours,
   I dream I am surrounded by the moons,
   All twenty-eight silvery pock-faced whores:
   The New and Old Moons, the in-between ones,
   The Full Moon broad and fat and weighing tons,
   The Dark Moon, the Black Moon which noone sees,
   A mummy of dried tar that love's mind shuns.
Their circle spins about me silver, green and gold.
I rush at what seems young and always grasp what's old,   *50*
More new than new, more old than old, the Black Moon cold,
A faggot-limbed, burlap-papped scarecrow stuffed with mould.

   My days, if they are days, are different too:
   I think we get our pleasure from grasping
   Difference and likeness; these I now eschew.
   I used to see a rat and then observe a robin,
   But now the bird seems but a rat with wings;
   A rose is but a rat without its legs, turned—
   Turned inside out to get the whites and pinks,
   A sunset's but a wide rat thoroughly burned,   *60*
   We geese are large rats stuck all over with feathers
A rat's breath cold & dry & hot & moist explains the winds and weathers,
So nothing has difference, therefore nothing is the same;
All things twin, all things opposed vanish in my doubt's marsh-flame.
Sometimes a nest of angels in the sun steal in my eyes like thieves.
I banish them by rolling on the ground in this suit of nettle-leaves.

Effie
   Branwell, our dreams are quite alike you know.
   My white wall is the moons that round you go.
   My garden is your glade where eight and score
   Torment a dying world that's lost its lore   *70*
   Of weaving into charms that shine a star,
   Nail whirlwinds and make spades of swords of war,
   Raise up the dead—the simple speakable air;
   And of my piping child you are the fallen heir.
   Branwell, I'll tell to you a curious tale

155

I once saw scratched upon a rusty pail
Thrown where the dungheaps in the barnyards start.
I spent the summer getting this by heart
And you too, Mopsus, listen if you must;
Women may also entertain the mind, I trust.   80
THERE was a Doorknob and a Door,
The former white and rather poor,
Yet handy for those going through
From hall to kitchen fro and to.
The door was made of solid pine,
Dark brown and varnished slick and fine;
'Doorknob!'said Door, 'you pale weak thing,
You spoil the look of me your king.
You dumbell clinging to my grandeur,
Asymmetry I can't endure.'   90

'Door, Door,' said Knob, 'What you are now
Is yet beyond my puzzling brow.
Your voice is like the sound of snow
Heard in mind of summer rainbow,
Or dumb seedless lumps of dark zinc
When green leaves try to on them think.
But though I cannot you define
I still know the successful line
To keep door, door—doorknob, doorknob:
To think by day is half my job,   100
To size up each approaching hand
And fit it with a surface bland;
I turn as smoothly as I can
To hand of wife and child and man;
When day is over then neap tide
Of dreams drowns all my day's neat pride;
Whales of Lust and Rays of Hate,
Madness like Eel and Fear like Skate
Swim rough and tumble in my mind;
Devouring all sane things they find   110
They warn me what net I must choose,
What hook & trident, leaden shoes,
Harpoons or cages I must use
When I do wake the following day
Beside the day-sea's voyage way
That leads through clouds of thoughts & hands
Unto again these dreamy sands
Where how to progress, how retreat
I learn for climbing world-life's street.'

'Leave off! Shut up!' shouted the Door,   120
'I'll not believe you any more.
You shouldn't have been to me tacked;
When I've lost you what have I lacked?
There! There!' The Door convulsed and shook
Knob snapped in two and Door forsook;
Rattling across two floors it rolled.

156

'Robbers!'. the farmer's wife carolled,
Awakening at the snapping sound.
Fierce as famished ravenous bloodhound
Farmer Smith sailed down the front stairs,   130
Night shirt flying, old hands flexed
To rid his house with robbers vexed.
Above the kitchen now his boys,
All five waked also with the noise.
Down like hail they came to kitchen
Tripping pails their ma kept swill in.
What thunder from the hallway where
Old Smith's loud crash does quake the air.
He misses knob and hits closed door.
His sons cry 'In the hall is robber!'   140
Crashing through door themselves they went
Through to hall and punch old gent,
Who bellows out with counter whack,
Pushing his five sons back, back, back.
Thus back and forth until the Door,
Crazed into splinters, was no more.
It lighted lamps for many a year,
Its knob was toy to children dear,
Still thinking, dreaming, showing them
How to be Ham, Japhet and Shem   150
And drunken Noah as all men must
Who for the height of being lust.

Mopsus
Ham, Shem, Drunken Noah? What does it mean?

Branwell
The meaning's felt often before it's seen;
My heart knows what my rusted mind does not.
Thank you, Effie. Such moments have I sought
When I might smile or pick at such a knot
As logic fingers could not ravel out at once.

Mopsus
I shall not sleep a wink thinking of this.
A sibyl come to out of her cave she is.   160
Perhaps we'll take you along to Mome Fair
To explain the merry-go-round there,
The ferris wheel & the sideshows to us.

Effie
But I always go to the fair, Mopsus,
And not one of these eggs but will be there too
Next September—for a general *nostalgie de la boue*.

APRIL

Argument

With Duncan as judge the geese hold a bardic contest in honour of Spring.

Duncan   Raymond   Valancy

Here is a kernel of the hardest winter wheat
Found in the yard delicious for to eat.
It I will give to that most poetic gander
Who this season sings as well as swam Leander.
The white geese with their orange feet on the green
Grass that grew round the pond's glassy sheen
Chose then Valancy and Raymond to sing
And to hear them gathered about in a ring.

Raymond
I speak I speak of the arable earth,
Black sow goddess huge with birth;   10
Cry cry killdeers in her fields.

Black ogress ate her glacier lover
When the sun killed him for her;
The white owl to the dark crow yields.

Caw caw whir whir bark bark
We're fresh out of Noah's Ark;
Wild geese come in arrowheads

Shot from birds dead long ago
Buried in your negro snow;
Long water down the river sleds.   20

Black begum of a thousand dugs,
A nation at each fountain tugs;
The forests plug their gaps with leaves.

Whet whet scrape and sharpen
Hoes and rakes and plows of iron;
The farmer sows his sheaves.

Mr. Sword or Mr Plow
Can settle in your haymow,
All is the same to Mother Ground.

Great goddess I from you have come,   30
Killdeer crow geese ditch leaf plowman
From you have come, to you return
In endless laughing weeping round.

Valancy
Your limbs are the rivers of Eden.
From the dead we see you return and arise,
Fair girl, lost daughter:
The swallows stream through the skies,
Down dipping water,
Skimming ground, and from chimney's foul dusk
Their cousins the swifts tumble up as the tusk   40
Of roar day
In bright May
Scatters them gliding from darkness to sun-cusp.

Your face unlocks the bear from his den.
The world has come into the arms of the sun.
What now sulky earth?
All winter you lay with your face like a nun,
But now bring forth
From river up boxdrain underground
Fish crawling up that dark street without sound   50
To spawn
In our pond
Young suckers and sunfish within its deep round.

Your body is a bethlehem.
Come near the sun that ripened you from earth
Pushing south winds
Through lands without belief till this pretty birth
The faithful finds:
Fanatic doves, believing wrens and orioles
Devoted redwinged blackbirds with their calls,   60
Archilochus alexandri,
Melospiza georgiana,
All surround you with arched cries of Love's triumphals.

Your mind is a nest of all young things, all children
Come to this meadow forest edge;
Put her together
From this squirrel corn dogtooth young sedge
And all this weather
Of the white bloodroots to be her skin
The wake robin to be her shin   70
Her thighs pockets
Of white violets
Her breasts the gleaming soft pearly everlasting.

For her limbs are the rivers of Eden;
Her face unlocks
The brown merry bear from his den,
From his box
The butterfly and her body is a bethlehem
Humming

With cherubim   80
And her mind is a cloud of all young things, all children.

The prize to this one goes cried eagerly some
And others cried that to Raymond it must come,
So that Duncan Goose turned to the plantain leaf
And chopped the prize in half with beak-thrust brief.

MAY

Argument

Effie and Fanny are discovered drynursing the entire flock of goslings.
Fanny describes how two propagandists recently roaming the
backwoods have met an interesting fate.

                Effie   Fanny

I think that yours will turn out white
    And mine will be the gray ones
But all just now are furry bright
    Like infant furry pocket suns.

Goslings now, goslings all
Run not near the muskrat's hall
Dancing weasel might prance up.

Yours will be white, mine will be gray,
    Some day now in the future,
But neither goose nor gander they   10
    Now play in tender nurture.

Goslings there, goslings dear
Swim not to those rushes near
Waiting skunk might on you sup.

Pray what's the news of snapping turtles
    And what of snapping foxes
We fend, we guard, we watch for rascals
    That snatch our goslings from us.

Fanny
To be worse for I heard from a cousin
    Who was down here loading caddises & cressing   20
That two strange geese of the scientific variety
        Had preached all year for their society,
    You do know how big the families are back there,
Forty-two or fifty-two goslings is not a thing rare.
        The section is so overpopulated,
    It puffs up and over with children inflated.
These two ladies want to save all the hill country women
        From all that labour and child-labouring.

160

'I've got the greatest news for you,' they juicy say,
To some farm wife who looks like a big five ring circus tent   30
    Held down by small children holding on it.
'We can show you how to stop this torment to-day,
We can show you how to stop conceiving & bearing children.'
    They open up their big black boxes then:
'This piece of straw, this frazzled bit of string, this old
Button from a castrati's overcoat at his death sold,
    Worth twenty babes any day and all free!'
Well, some places they caused a riot jamboree,
And some other places the people didn't catch on what
    They meant. 'To bring forth children never not—   40
Who now could want that desert barren state?' they said.
'But you could have one or plan for two, plump & decent fed
    And warmly clothed,' these smooth ladies rejoined.
'You then could buy yourself a kill-yourself-if-you-touch-it
And a watch-everybody-squeeze-up-from-hell-while-you-sit;
An electric jelly-fish warmer than a husband to go to bed with you
And a pass-like-a-vulture-shadow and get your sons to do
Two-backed tricks in the back and flatten 5,000,000 frogs too.'
    'But,' said the people, 'we like having more, once joined;
And one doesn't raise as well as a dozen and a half.   50
    You grow us more food and wages, smarty;
Meanwhile we'll keep hoeing our own kindergarty.
Just how could one huge cow rest its heart on one little calf?
    Children are our life, our bread and our clothing,
With their two little arms & legs & their one head
They come toppling shouting out of us to prove we're not dead.
    Can God not damn you for hating being?'
Now then the two biddies came to the conclusion
After a year of very little success that pretty soon
    They'd have to go back when one night they met   60
Coming up a hill toward them two handsome yet
Sort of grim rakish sly curly young men who looked just like.
    'Why you slick ladies aren't going farther
In this wet and no-dry-hotel-for-miles weather?'
'We can suffer far more than this for the cause of no-tyke.
    The more it rains on us, the more we laugh,
It can't wet us with what we waxy know; we scoff
At rain and suffer to decrease humanity: we're glad
To outwit any fertility.' The two brothers bade
    Them come for food & shelter to their house.   70
They went, more than slightly attracted, to this place.
It was old, mossy roofed & gabled with many windows
    Set between leafy thick appletree rows.
The brothers asked these expert girls to be their wives.
First these spinsters said not by the beard of their chinny lives.
    At length to a ceaseless mad tattooing
Of caresses they allowed the brothers' wooing
And made their special preparations for the bridal night.
    They tied the brothers up in sheets of tight
Glass, beaten gold, cork, rubber, netting, stoppers, sand;   80

161

They themselves dammed their wombs with a pretty skillful hand
     And lay back waiting for the sensation
Of an interesting lively copulation,
Without any of the disfiguring after effects necessary for population.
     Nevertheless and oh nevertheless
The brothers so handled their part of the process
That in six weeks' time the ladies in question were with child,
     Seeded down by those strange men dark & wild.
'How on earth did you do this to us, Roderick?'
They groaned & shrieked & roared. 'And you too, dreadful Benedict!'   9
     'Madams, we are twins,' the brothers explained,
'And for centuries our old family has gained
New members for itself always in twos or threes or fours.
     Our emblem is a white sow with twelve pigs
All sucking her dry, like bishops in periwigs
All translating at a Holy Bible, and you we picked
     To test our fertile power on since you kicked
Our family's sense of lively birth in the teeth.
From this day may you billow saw waddle gag groan beneath
     The ripeness of a Nile in bringing forth!'   1
A dark cloud swept thunderously down from the North
Of snapping turtles, newts & hopping toads; as in a dream
     The women's loins poured forth a swollen stream
Until the brothers moved them to their granary
Where they were turned into strong & sturdy machinery;
     One into a large & squat fanning mill,
The other to a tall conical cylindrical
Iron Maiden used for threshing seeds from ripe sunflowers.
So usefully did end the lives of those insistent life devourers.

JUNE

Argument

*Branwell is still suffering from Dorcas' defection. A huge gray owl
seems always to be taunting him.*

    Mopsus Branwell

Now is the ox-eyed daisy out
     Out now everywhere,
The bobolink tips his wings
In the humming blue gold air.

The wild rose opens simple eyes
     In a green briar face,
The mourning dove beats a drum
In a drowsy shady place.

The strawberry like a wren's heart
Shows beneath three green leaves,   10

The garter snake leaves behind
One of his silver glittering crystal annual sleeves.

Branwell, where have you wandered now
That seem as sad as snow on bough
And can't look like the time.
What can be better than this weather—
The wind made out of red clover
The clouds as white as rime.

Branwell
I have been shooting with my gun
At a bird that eats my sun;   20
It seems a hooting owl
Large, moping, gravid, dismal, gray.
I saw it flit beneath a dray
That large sad dreary fowl
But when I shot it out of this
It flew unharmed up with a hiss
Onto a shadowy beam.
And when I shot again it flew
Out to blight the fields' green hue
Into the gray of dream.   30
Whereafter this ash bird threw back
My leaden bullets of attack
Solemnly laughing then.
My friend, I now give up the fight
Endless as that of day and night
And stand accursed among men.

Mopsus
My father knew of such a bird,
It made all life seem edgeless, blurred
And sat upon his head
Fouling his shoulders and his hair,   40
Raising its young in that strange lair
And vomiting up the dead.
He never stirred to shoo it off
But waited late and long enough
Until it sank from sight.
Soft answered did its wrath dissolve
And sink into the gay revolve
Of his thoughts so light.
He looks a little like an owl
But still is human, toe to jowl,   50
And merrier than ever.
To fight that bird were downright folly
For her name is Melancholy.

Branwell
No, I cannot patient your advice,
I can only twist in the hard vise

163

Of her betrayal.
She took my presents all to him,
She gave him all her treasure slim
While talking our betrothal.
This found I lately in a lost   60
Letter in the orchard grass.
The small bur basket that I stuck together for her
She left out in the rain until unstuck.
When she would hardly let me take her arm
She gave her beak entire to that gross buck.

   I am like a hollow tree
Where the owl & weasel hide
   I am like a hollow tree
Dead in the forest of his brothers.

   My feet are sensitive as brains   70
Put hats upon them
   My feet are sensitive as brains
All the ground is grassed with knives.

   These fingers that once played
Nimbly the harp
   These fingers that once played
Are soft & suck as leeches.

   My throat where once a song
Flew out like a golden bird
   My throat where once a song   80
Is a woodpecker's bitten door.

   My eyes are the entrances
To the kingfishers' nests
   My eyes are the entrances
Tunnels of clay lined with fish bones.

   I see the red sun sink
For the last time this far north.
The full moon rises: my thoughts fly forth.
Leap forth, oh bird of prey & turncoat ermine,
   Nebula out of my mind   90
     That swampy fair
Where the bittern pumps from its cistern of despair.

JULY

Argument

Valancy & Anser compare methods of educating the young goslings. Anser is their schoolmaster.

Anser   Valancy

Hohum there, Valancy. What brings you down to the gosling school?

Valancy
Well, I went to the granite boulder in the pasture and I found you weren't there. When I was a gosling, Old Strictus sometimes held the school in the hollow where there used to be a cabin but you weren't there either. Why have you moved the school to this boggy acre?

Anser
The goslings voted that we move it here. The crickets are very plentiful hereabouts and so are the young frogs and lizards.

Valancy
Indeed you are different from my old teacher. He alone had the vote in our school and if we didn't come to school he searched us out from the grass in which we were hiding with a strong thrumming dig of his old yellow beak.

Anser
You cannot educate the young goslings by fear. Nor by breaking their will; you must persuade them to prefer herdsgrass to bladder campion. You should not beak the child.

Valancy
I like what you say. Where are your students by the way?

Anser
It's the boy's fault. He's told to watch us you know, but look at him. He has fallen asleep as indeed I did myself. When he's asleep my students steal into the fields of pease and buckwheat and gorge themselves to their heart's content. Don't frown at that. They are happy. Let them be happy.

Valancy
Well Anser, I agree that you should persuade rather than force them. But I don't think that applies to their attendance. I mean surely they must be here, or how can you persuade them?

Anser
You are rather conventional in your views and I think you will soon realize that you are attacking a good thing. You'll soon see, I think, that the rule does indeed apply even to their attendance. You see the subject I teach them is taught to them even when they are not here—not

165

physically present.

Valancy
Good Lord! What do you teach them?

Anser
Now first, my friend, whatever did that pedagogue of such renown, Old Strictus, teach you as a gosling?

Valancy
When I was a gosling he taught us to know the most wonderful list of things. You could play games with it; whenever you were bored or miserable what he had taught you was like a marvellous deck of cards in your head that you could shuffle through and turn over into various combinations with endless delight. At the end of the year we each made ourselves little huts of burdock leaves, lay down on our backs with large stones on our bellies and recited the whole thing over to ourselves forwards and backwards. Some of the poorer students were in those huts till November but even those to whom it was an agony, when they at length did know that they knew all that a young goose was supposed to know, the moment when they rolled the stone away and climbed out of their burdock hut—it was as joyous a moment as if they had been reborn into another world.

Anser
Well, well, well. Might I ask just what this reviving curriculum was?

Valancy
 Who are the children of the glacier and the earth?
 Esker and hogsback, drumlin and kame.
 What are the four elements and the seven colours,
 The ten forms of fire and the twelve tribes of Israel?
 The eight winds and the hundred kinds of clouds,
 All of Jesse's stem and the various ranks of angels?
 The Nine Worthies and the Labours of Hercules,
 The sisters of Emily Brontë, the names of Milton's wives?
 The Kings of England and Scotland with their Queens,
 The names of all those hanged on the trees of law
 Since this province first cut up trees into gallows.
 What are the stones that support New Jerusalem's wall?
 Jasper and sapphire, chalcedony, emerald,
 Sard, sardius, chrysolite, beryl, topaz,
 Chrysoprasus, hyacinthine and amethyst.

Anser
My goodness, how useless so far as the actual living of life is concerned. Why we have simplicity itself compared to what that maze of obscurity was. I mean since our heads are going to be chopped off anyhow we only teach the young gosling what he likes.

Valancy
We liked what Strictus taught though it took some effort.

Anser
Pah! If they like nothing, then teach them that. The self must be free.

AUGUST

Argument

*Raymond chances upon a famous critic-goose's funeral. Whose ghost
actually appears: apparently it has been raised after a bout of its
favorite activity—putting poems into order of merit.*

Raymond Lobo Blot Busto Terpsichore Scrutumnus

Is not this trenchant Lobo? Is not
This Busto and Mr Amos Blot?
Surely these are the nine Muses
And these the Furies with lighted fuses
And these the Graces one taking, two giving—
All mourning one no longer living
But dead within his pale blue coffin,
A child perhaps no longer laughing.
Ah! what a crowd of mourners here
All dressed in black each with his tear.   10

Lobo
Go bid the soldiers shoot
Go bid each screech owl hoot
For Scrutumnus he is dead
Who contained in his wee head
A sharper sense of good and bad
Than all the ages' gooses had.

Blot
Go bid the women shriek and cry.
Go bid them black their dresses dye.
He who first showed how to choose
Between the fast, between the loose,   20
The connoisseur of crickets' songs
Who knew his harps and knew his gongs
Died ere his precious work was done.
Died and veiled with tar our sun.

Busto
The song of gull and hawk and shrike
He first discovered, first did like.
The fancy wren, the too sweet lark
He bravely thrust down into dark.
The language of the common sparrow,
The music of the untaught farrow   30
Held he sweeter far than thrushes
Whistling silver trills and rushes.

167

Pigs and sparrows sing 'We copulate,'
And mean exactly what they state.

Raymond
Egad! Who was this Tamburlaine,
Who said bluebirds sing like a chilblain
And made old reputations fall
Like feathery snow from Mother Holl.

Lobo
Scrutumnus! Scrutumnus! Scrutumnus!
We lay this wreath on thy tumulus!   40
A wreath of thy favourite pigsweed
And lambsquarters gone to seed.
Bring on the songs and we will play
His favourite game upon this day.

Blot
Ladies and gentlemen, after I've sung
These three songs from my leather lung
Establish a preference among the three,
But evaluate judiciously.

The First Song
Snort we and grunt we, love,
  Pigs in the sties of Venus   50
The fairest pair e'er transformed, love,
  For Circe's circus.

Swink we and sweat we, sweet,
  Guzzling our julep amorous
From the great she-wolf's teat
  A strange Remus & Romulus.

Though we puppets dally
  'Tis the theatre of a god;
Though this pintel rudely rally
  What puts it out—a lotus pod.   60

Clapclapclapclapclapclapclapclap

The Second Song
Like to a dewdrop was thy love to me
That glitters sweetly in the morn's new light,
Fairer than any in that jewelled sea
Fastened upon the bank's high bosky height.

Alas, when I had climbed your face to sight
Through all the prickets' grasping stings & snags,
I found that you had long since taken flight
Enamoured of my rival's golden bags.

168

Clapclapclapclap   70

The Third Song
Rubicund cherub, thy wings waft
Star planets clouds kingdoms past;
My cordial soul its humid clout
Ignite and set ablaze.

Blue vivid seraph with thy wand
Glittering with golden words inscribed
Promiscuous and tangled
  Mnemonically wave.

Candid Spirit, pure as the Sun of Sun
Come, oh come O Angel with a pen,   80
Inhabit this prepared twelve-tribed den
Thy cradled, crossed and rising
  Song to bring forth.
Hmh.
Now quickly without conferences
Hand in the noted preferences.
Erato here prefers the first, I see,
And you the second, fond Melpomene;
Why Urania, you have liked the third!
Shortly before his death Scrutumnus heard   90
And judged these songs; the first!
By John Dong he adjudged the first!
The second by Edmund Lily Goose
Comes second! he said he found it loose
With no real emotion urging it on,
The images overdecorous and overdrawn.
The third he found obscure, a farrago
Of bad English and worse Latin lingo,
No real emotion, no language of the people,
Immoral in its basic avoidance of simplicity,   100
Pompous overblown fantastically . . .

Terpsichore
But you and Scrutumnus, sir, do not
Understand these songs. One ought
To see that each has a different purpose
And therefore a different word choice,
You do not laugh at a cat or a frog
Because they cannot act like a hog.

Blot
I do, madam. You are wrong, wench!

Lobo
Who's this skirted lesbian stench?

169

Busto
Take her prisoner! Tie her down. 110
We'll give her a green gown.
Give me my pruning hook & sword cane.
Now where my shadow falls on this bane
I'll spare, but where it does not fall
I'll cut an offering for his funeral.

Raymond
Your shadow is much shorter than her form.

Lobo
Then she must bow to him, for he's the norm.

Raymond
Which will he cut? Her head or her feet?

Busto
I'll cut her head. Here Nymph so fleet,
In dancing your abominations 120
Dance no more on the honest man's sensations.
Nymph of Sciolism, my honest shears convect,
My desire is constative with my effect!

Raymond
Fortunately noone can kill a Muse
Unless their own to kill they choose.
To kill his own genius is all he can do.
What is this unmelodious hullabaloo
And smell of sulphur? Scrutumnus, Thou!

*The Shade Of Scrutumnus**
Aooh! Bow wowwowwowwowwowwow

Raymond
Why little man what is this harp you have here 130
With a spider in it?

The Shade
            Mine! Mine, do you hear?
And noone shall take it from me!

---

*The critical judgements of Scrutumnus are deservedly famous. Once on being shown a great marble palace of exquisite beauty, he exclaimed, 'That little outhouse across the way has more real sincerity.' When first told the story of the little princes in the Tower he exclaimed how much they must have got on Richard III's nerves and how dark passionate energies were to be preferred to stagnant frozen purities. Often his friends' mouths fell open at the audacity and the courage his determination to speak out entailed. When a person in the goosehouse was showing forth the wonders of the universe—the stars, the Milky Way, mountains, etc., he complained that the Universe was needlessly

SEPTEMBER

Argument

In the farmhouse world Peter & Ann get married just in time: in the
goose world you see Mome Fair as our geese see it. There are exhibits of
prize animals & plants, the rides, a remarkable funhouse, sideshows
and a preacher who is roaring drunk. George & Dorcas particularly
liked the ferris wheel, Mopsus the merry-go-round, Effie the sideshows
and Branwell went into the funhouse again & again for another look at
the horse-eating iris.

By parents strong pegged young Peter and Ann
Were wedded in welter by waspish minister.
Home had they hugged huge bride with child
When wonder! wonder! wawled soon infant;
Ceremony, wed-supper, then son and heir.
Haw haw such haste, hiccoughed the gathering . . .

MOME FAIR

The Blind Fiddler plays just inside the gate
The Pouter Pigeon
               proudly pouts at window,
Crozier and cap and scarlet carillon.   10
Heretic helmet dove's hearse rolls up,
'Stone it shakers! Stone it my doves!'
Peevishly primps out Pouter Pigeon stiff,
But barbs brotherly bury poor heretic,
Coat with concrete his coffin fearing that
Pouter Pigeon may perhaps pry him up.
Beautiful boomchested Bishop Pouter
Commands croppers to carve out other graves,
Fetch the faithful finikins to new place,
Sell this site to slaked-lime makers,   20
Confident of course that the concrete's tough.

The Cat
Gracious gracious gallant galvanizing puss
Sleek satin hide and secretion eyes:

---

obscure and he rather wondered if God had simply not played an
elaborate joke on us all. 'I think God gathered a little coterie around him
of admiring sycophantic angels who praised whatever he did,' said
Scrutumnus, 'no matter how hideously entangled.' But his most famous
critical mot was his judgement of God's Tiger: looking at it very, very
closely and making some sensitive observations on the beauty of the
stripe work he said—turning to the hind legs—that it was too bad after
such a splendid beginning that God had scamped the conclusion of this
noble creation. Someone asked him what he meant by this; he said,
'Why can't you see? The hind legs are almost identical with the front
legs. He has merely repeated the first idea for the front legs, and has
not been able to work out a proper conclusion to his work at all.'

In the morn innocent indecent exposure,
PM perambulates puckishly pussies in restaurants,
Corrosive urine crackles in crazed urinal,
Dim bannisters dally his dumpling dairy maid,
Yowls he in Yonge Street of yare conquest . . .
Postcoit pining pans him to early bed,
But TWO finds him tootling untiringly meeow flute.   30

The Dog
    Feisty fugleman, frowsy small dog
    Yipped and yapped and yowled and growled,
    Teasing travellers on track of blessing quest,
    Lifted a leg at lustrous silk parasols,
    Slept when the silky sage thief came tripping,
    Disgusted the dewy white damsel Moon.

The Pig
    Pink protrusion, pachyderm pork crystal,
    Crackling with conch sounds casual acorn;
    Mice muzzle and masticate your back
    Unbeknownst by unquick ununquiet mind;   40
    Hear nothing ears except earhasp twitch,
    Smell nothing snout except swine incense,
    Touch nothing trotters save tapioca stye wallow:
    Eyes examine the excellent nose horizon,
    Heedless of huntsmen horning your oak hall,
Dreaming of the devoured peacock safe down in your belly.

The Hen
    Hohum humble hiked herself to Sunday School,
    Never nudged neck up to sky,
    Looked late & soon longingly downward,
    Found foody scraps, fetched them to others,   50
    Dug in the dunghill—her delight by the hour,
    Pecked not the pants of the puerile kicker,
    Rebuked not the ribald rooster's oppressions,
    Stood the steal-weasel's sucking all eggs of hers,
    Forgave the fox for chewing her wing,
    Fine eggs, fair feathers, fat carcass, old hen.

The Cow
    Fanciful flighty fairy cow,
    Black & white bulging beautiful thing.
    Burdock bites she busily out of barn door,
    Slavers till sicked over salt block at gate.   60
    New grass assaulted at stone boat by her,
    Cagily corn she corrals over barbed wire,
    Tree leaves tassel out twitching mouth,
    New clover now navigates she through gate,
    Gorges down googols of juicy green fodder,
    Bloats her four bellies up balloonwise-zeppelin,
    Mooing for mercy meanders to keeper-help

Who sticks her with sharp pen, soon rush out
All vapours as velvety voluptuous tongue darts
Out again.   *70*

The Closed Gentian
    Gentlefolk gentian purple gentleman flower
    First prize finds fuzzy buzz seekers after gold,
    Golden manners, golden heart, golden gold cellar-hidden;
    Cellar-kept, for closed gentian cruelly stays shut,
    Shut, shut shameless hand, shamble-soul plant:
    Traps robber tumbled in tenacious for honey:
    Stinking beauty, star-hell sterile-pregnant gentian.

AMPERSAND the ewe, mare, cock and drake, rose caterpillar and cheese.

Dante's Inferno & Funhouse

Rivière du Loup 1. A huge gasping gaping jaw narrowing to rapids.

Castor grassus 2. A small room padded with beaver fur.

Montreal 3. A room painted with demon faces, arms holding out

Niagara Falls white dogs, drums beating, rushing roaring sound.

Louis XV 4. A shower of milk and a swarm of honeybees.*

5. Freezing cold passage way, lamprey eels pursued by

Moraviantown Latvians; an old Indian's skin is turned into horse-whips and shoelaces, deafening explosion.

Mackenzie 6. A bloody divan wearing a lace fichu awaits you in this room.

Dawson Road 7. Go fast through this steam chamber where a Red Nose†

Batoche glowing confronts an Eye‡ glaring. A White Horse is also having quite a time with a monster horse-eating iris which

Regina has NEVER FORGET printed on its petals. A pouter pigeon struts by.

8. This room seems like a railway carriage running on a

Craigellachie monorail attached to the crotches of a row of bearded gentlemen all standing in a row with tophats on.

Laurier 9. You are smoking a pipe; the conductor says, 'Defense de fumer.'

1912 10. A Tiger yowls by with a lady on his back.**

11. The train comes to grief in a drift of flourdough.

12. You stumble into a room where a man is being tre-panned: a lineup of 100,000 are all waiting to be in

1914 deathly silence. Accompanying you is a pale beaver type: everyone has him. He is continually telling you to duck ghost cobwebs.

13. A horrible smell fills the room: every time the atten-

---

*Anointment with milk and honey was part of French coronation rites.
†Macdonald.
‡Riel.
**The election was fought over reciprocity with the U.S.A. A favourite opposition poster.

173

1937	dants try to turn on ventilating fans a group of stately voices say, 'No. You are interfering with the right to smell.'††
	14. Another room lined with freshly bleeding scalps. A
1942	small spiral tunnel, rather messy, leads you to a beach where sea serpents and glass bubbles float towards you. These disappear and you are back at the fair again steppin
Port Moody	over a dead warrior with flaxen hair who must have tried to get in the wrong way and going by a simply exhausted old harridan in a cage who is trying to sell tickets to it.

The Merry-Go-Round

Out of French chivalry comes an endless string of gracefully up and downing wooden horses all pursuing a brass ring labelled TRUTH and it is TRUTH. Loafkneaders and genitalmen, I will describe to you these jumping up and down beasts as they sail by. I; we have here a really stock

Parmenides still stoneheavy big Percheron that does not go up and down like the others because as a matter of fact he doesn't believe in it. II; a fiery steed! it goes up and down like

Heraclitus nothing but and its whole form keeps flowy-changing; as a matter of fact you can't seem to sit in the same saddle twice on it it seems. III; here's a beautiful white horse— peculiar—it's got a beeyootiful glass horse sailing above it

Plato and the horse you're sitting on keeps looking up in the most sort of ridiculous way trying to do exactly what the glass horse is doing but of course it just looks like a cheap imitation particularly since it keeps looking up all the time and the beautiful glass horse has such poise it never looks anywhere except straight ahead. IV; a rather stocky Clydesdale with three saddles, three heads and three but-

Aristotle tocks: one buttock is too hairy, the middle one is just right and the left hand one has no hair at all. V; just behin

Democritus him is a very shifty galloway—all sand as a matter of fact, all whirling around and you're in danger of sinking into your saddle up to your topknot. VI; here's a drunken old

Epicurus nag with a wreath of poppies slung about its neck. VII; a sorry nag with its bottom up in the air because it's sub-

Zeno duing its bottom and that's the surest way of tiring your bottom out. Its skin is all leathery; it leathers it by beating it against the walls of its stall so that if anyone *should* bea you see, why it wouldn't feel this at all. VIII; next we have a horse looking extremely thoughtful—no wonder his

St. Augustine rear quarters are half pitch dark and half blinding white and no amount of dye will ever get the beast either one colour or the other. There's a certain marionette like

---

†† 'The Judicial Committee of the Privy Council judicially condemned virtually any national plan to cope with any Canadian depression.' Creighton, *Dominion of the North.* In short, Bennett's New Deal interfered with the right of the provinces to be depressed.

174

quality about this horse's prancing as if every capriole
were destined by some other force than the horse's mind.
This horse wears a certain self satisfied look on his face as
if he knew a secret nightmare noone else did. IX; a very
fat round mare slops by looking as if she bore twin foals,

Aquinas one maybe a classic stallion and the other a milkwhite
unicorn filly unified within her. Well, let her amble by.
X; trotting behind her is a lean pale horse who smirks at

Duns Scotus her girth and completeness and seems to wear always a
knowing look as if let's not talk about a full manger laid
up in heaven when work is over but let's have a look at
just a wisp of hay here right in front of me. XI; what a
pretty snow white horse tattooed with stars, mountains

Boehme meadows real sheep moving on them it seems & fiery
comets & ships in a harbour & little horses dancing in a
barnyard. This horse's eyes—oh the angelic aurora wonder of its gold red mane. Every once in a while this
horse's colour completely changes. People shy away then
I can tell you! Storms break out in the tattooed skies and a
fiery fire burns in the eyes. However, it bubbles over—a
light comes into his eyes and the world changes back again.
XII; now here comes a smart little fossil horse large as a

Descartes fox ticking as if it worked mechanically with melted
beeswax in its feedbag and a distinctly mathematical looking hoof (it could add I'm sure if it were let loose) as well
as a tendency to go for weighty things like lumps of coal
you may hand him: but he doesn't go for painted butterflies or candy sugar sticks. XIII; a brutish nasty and short

Hobbes small fat merrylegs of a pit pony speckled all over with
the pitchings of flies. XIV; and next a foundered staggered
old thing—covered with boils, rather agonized and heavy

Heidegger looking as if it might leap for the sky. No wonder—
Merrylegs has his teeth in his hind quarters. But, my
goodness, I believe it's the horse we started out with, only,
since we saw it last it may have changed a bit you see what
with the merry-go-round going around you see.

The Ferris Wheel
When you're on it you don't notice this phenomenon but by that time
you're a clown enjoying your pastime:* right now we are learneds and
we are enjoying the puzzle of the ferris wheel. As the baskets come
round you see that this one is like a whole landscape suspended from
two chains with (a) agricultural types dancing about a factory chimney
(b) out of a bush wildly excited louts chase wild man dressed up in a
skin of thick green painted leaves.

Basket Two contains (a) bonfire (b) men and women dancing about
this (c) changing into a wheel which is dipped in pitch, set afire and set
whirling like a huge sunflower down the green mountain (d) this wheel

---

*A paraphrase of something Sir James Frazer says in *The Golden
Bough*. The Ferris Wheel turns through that book.

gets smaller but pretty soon it's up on top of the hill again as big as ever (e) look close and you can still see the men and women dancing around like seeds forming in the fire blossoms.

What does the third basket contain? Answer: (a) a circle of reapers in a field of deadripe wheat who are rapidly come closer together in their circle until in the last knot of uncut grain a furious bird hisses up, sometimes a goose, a cat, a pig, even a little man (b) the bird escapes underneath the reapers' legs who pursue him with their scythes, binders and threshing machines and kill him (c) then they eat him. But next year the bird will still be there in the last sheaf of grain.

Basket Four reveals an inverted spring world: (a) it's November (b) through the trees of this wood I see stags leaping up into the air with forests on their heads. Of course it is their spring for it's the rutting season. Our dancers have lit a bonfire and some are leaping through it. People come to the fire with faggots and march away eyes of flame polkadotting the dark forest farther and farther away thereafter.

On a snowy ground in Basket Five men and women have catscradles in their hands which they keep changing from hand to hand into various patterns (a running man, a sunflower, an angry bird, a leaping deer, a wawling child): other dancers arrive beating drums, frying pans, sieves, kettles, their own heads until the stars fade, the snow disappears and out of the ground push the green claws & yellow horns and red tongues of a bonfire.

The next basket shows a happy child surrounded by men in wolf masks. A green wreath on his head, he is shaking a noisemaker and a rattle in his hands; on a pebble in front of him there is propped up a mirror, a present from his stepmother.

And the last basket contains the Sun and the Moon themselves with fat round bodies and faces beaming. The Moon has a dozen or so gray hound-dogs in her arms and her lap: these are the ragged clouds she hunts with on stormy nights. Between her left hand & his right hand extends a web or catscradle of the tides and winds, rivers, fountains and whirlwinds which these two are continually changing into other patterns. The moon looks domestic here; as a matter of fact, she is continually escaping from the sun and her wanderings are recorded in spiral tattoo marks upon his left arm. By consulting these he knows where she has got to in her wanderings and when he will next be able to meet her face to face, he in the East and she in the West. In his left hand he holds a cage with a bird in it which represents the times they meet: like a falcon this bird is often sent out to search for her. This cage resembles a lantern.

The Caterpillar Ride
Goes round and opens up its dusky dusty top: infants look out hardening and changing into old men & women; the brown hood closes down, goes round, opens up, young children looking out and so on.

The Sideshows
Thunder, thunder & deal out light, darkness, Heaven-shell, Earth, Sea, plants, Sun & Moon, fishes, birds (whirr!) animals (grr!) and man and

176

then all history with its gaudy banners stretches out down a lane in front of you: the banners glazed with the streaming rain although it could just be lice in the crotch and armpits and hair of creation. The first bunch of sideshow tents—after the exhibit of a huge whale on blocks of salt* which literally stinks to high heaven—are black. Inside you will see a dancing bear, a girl with Russell's viper, a talking crow with a split tongue that can read your hand, Siamese twins, a Cyclops, a four legs, a three arms, a no legs, a notable criminal pickled in a glass case on display. The second bunch are white tents: banners promise you the daughter of Chief White Man; she is a tremendous bearded fat woman the size of Mars' biggest moon at least; a dozen girls who take their clothes off, a man throwing a cloud of knives at a girl. In the yellow tents—shooting galleries, hooptoss, wheels of Fortune, a waxwork show with a torture chamber containing the Seven Steps to Heaven.

The last red tents contain a man in a sphere on a motorcycle, stilt walkers, fire eaters, sword swallowers, a talking pelican, a tremendous eagle, a man who gets in and out of a suitcase, and last of all the Grotto of the Beautiful Hermaphrodite.

The Drunken Preacher
      Lo, it was the last supper, I leader from gutter
      Tell you tall and short tinkery folks gathered.
      What did those white souls eat while their Lord talked:
      I don't know indeed I don't, maybe sandwiches.
      And He said haughtily head up to the twelve,
      'I'll ask you assafoetidae again I will,
      Isn't there one, one disciple with the spunk to betray me?'
      They all fumbled their food, fed themselves slowly.
      'Otherwise you see all my work ought in value is.'
      'I will,' quavered weakly woefully poor Judas,
      Runty little redhaired man runaway parents from him.
      'I'll go through with ghoulish Holy Ghost necessary job.'
      Even then at the end of it elder tree saw he.
      His death, his Lord's death held him at Lord's supper.
      So you've all certainly betrayed him so you've done
      Something for him by my bottle faith fiddle de dee you have.

      Threshing machine still threshes throat-drying chaff;
      Sun with its sperm belt spangles against cog moon,
      Fat horses at farm fetch the wheel round & round,
      In the rain-mud runcible 'aroint thee' bubbling.
      They haul out from high loft, fork handfuls of pea straw
      Beneath bashing horsehooves.
      Little babe loudly screams, last thunder of year.

---

*A whale was exhibited in this way throughout Ontario some time during the thirties.

OCTOBER

Argument

Branwell sings a very autumnal song; he has never recovered from the disastrous affair with Dorcas. His nettle suit has turned brown and dry with age.

Raymond   Branwell

Sing to us for the frost
  Is closing the pond,
The elms their leaves have lost
And the singing birds have gone.

Branwell
What can I sing to you?
  I have a song
Perhaps it will do,
I found it at the Fair.

GREEN grove walk toward me,
    Around me with   10
      That which
Trembles heartsmith.

Currant tinkle bobbob
  Pheasant leap whir
      Squirrel
A pink mushroom, sir!

Little missy white violets
  Squirrel corn
      Bloodroots
Bossy lost her horn.   20

As yet not boxes
  Gallows
    Legs, pulpits
Of trees windblows.

Hollow tree tuwhoos
  Come here
    Mousie
And robin redbreast dear.

Far away red faraway
  Red as fire   30
    A fox
Flash and transpire.

I met a green woman:
Her feet were paths
Her eyes were bunchberries
Her arms elm lathes
Her tongue a mushroom
Her teeth white violets
Her nose an owl feather,
Her mouth like cressets.   40

Did I touch her?
   Vanished.
      Twang!
Garnisheed

All pulse-wage since
   And this place
Holds my heart in a bottle
   Of pathpace.

Raymond
This song is like the grapes now
   Black in the arbours of fences,   50
Wild apples from their lane bough
   Savage and sweet to the senses.

Nailed and studded are the quietnesses
   With wrinkled dark butternuts,
Prickly beechnuts of brown darknesses,
   Ripe burs' pinch and hook and clutch.

The shorter sun sets farther south,
   The foxes are about now,
The wind whistles with a narrow mouth,
Up to the gooseshed we had better go.   60

NOVEMBER

Argument

*Four birds discuss the calendar. Mopsus has certainly come a long way
from the detachment & 'calm canals' he mentioned at first.*

> *Ookpik   Starling   Wildgoose   Mopsus*

Birdies, can there be any doubt
My master, Winter, turns the wheel,
   The Miller whom none love.
I at the spindle pole have been
And through the swarming shuddering snow
   Seen at work the God of Death;
Winter and Death turn all the world,

179

Man and continents come apart
　　Like skin from flesh from bone.
The world was planned in cold arithmetic,　　　　　*10*
Numbers flapping like vultures fast & thick
Down and around my merry Master Zero
Like birds of prey about a stone dead hero.

Starling
　　The year begins when it grows warm;
　　Then I once more do mate and chirp
　　　　And fly out from the town.
　　It is not year or time at all
　　When all there's eatable is dung
　　　　And all is frozen round.
　　Give me the eaves of a steam laundry　　　*20*
　　Where I dream of upperworld spring
　　　　Above this grave of cold.
Once I lived in a place of sun,
I wish I knew how there to run,
Migrationless I debris am
Yet know the world begins with warm.

Wildgoose
　　My wings tell me that September*
　　Shall the year's beginning be;
　　　　Up those wide rungs I climb
　　And fly a vigorous sabbath south　　　　*30*
　　And find no winter in my year
　　　　But live a summer seesaw;
　　Two summers like a figure eight
　　Two wings like tables of the law
　　　　Are my four seasons.
The wobbling earth with its Goliath snows
I steady and defeat with feathered blows.
The year begins when death and chaos sprout
And I must with a new world beat them out.

Mopsus
　　A sun, a moon, a crowd of stars,　　　　*40*
　　A calendar nor clock is he
　　　　By whom I start my year.
　　He is most like a sun for he
　　Makes his beholders into suns,
　　　　Shadowless and timeless.
　　At the winter sunstill some say
　　He dared be born; on darkest day
　　　　A babe of seven hours
He crushed the four proud and great directions
Into the four corners of his small cradle.　　　*50*

---

* The Jews begin their year in September.

180

He made it what time of year he pleased, changed
Snow into grass and gave to all such powers.

DECEMBER

Argument

*Most of the geese are executed. Those geese to be saved are marked off
with marking rings on their legs. Branwell's is taken from him by
George, but Effie willingly gives hers up. She prefers to help Branwell
face the block & also to go with him into the new dimension she hopes
awaits them after death. We leave the goosehouse, the farmhouse and
finally enter our own world again.*

Day of wrath and terror came now!
Chop chop chop chop chop
The farmers killed their geese for Christmas market.
Each day Peter came and took a dozen
Held their feet with one hand and with other
Brought down the axe that severs dreading heart
From dreading mind; Mopsus went first
And suffered stubbornly running about
The yard for minutes without his head.
Some said, 'Care for my little mouse,' and some   10
Said what a small slender neck it was;
Others, 'The gods themselves weep o'er such dooms,'
Or, 'Goose Grease! what crimes are done in thy name.'
The cats and dogs ran away with their heads,
Betty and Ann then plucked off their feathers,
Stoppered their necks with brown paper and tied
Their legs together ready for market stall.
Betty chose Branwell and Dorcas, Effie, Valancy
And Old Keziah to keep the race alive.

George

      Help! Help! He's choosing those without the rings.   20
      They put the rings on you to mark you off.
      Give me your ring! Why bother saving you?
      Ow! These nettles sting. I'm the buck
      That'll keep the race alive for them.

Branwell

      Well, what do I do now? Wait for Peter I guess.
      I'd hardly realized what the rings were for.

Effie

      Who could be glad to be left alive, who could
      Cling to this cramped stupid goosehouse world.
      For 'Death's the green pathway' to the fields of Life
      'Die would we daily once it to expert.'   30
      Help me off with this pink marking ring.

Fanny, see if it will fit your leg.
Who knows, at the very least we become men
When we die. Take off the suit of nettles
Of our selves. Here, Branwell, listen to the ring
You think might save your life. What does it sound like?

Branwell

It's the merry-go-round at the fair
Or the ferris wheel far far far away.

Effie

Life inside of that is a crazed prison
Of despair. You can't possibly want it.   40

Branwell

I can't help it, I'm afraid, I want the ring.
I can't see a path that leads between one's
Head & one's body.

Effie

                When you are changed then
One arm may always remain a goose wing.

On Christmas Day at farmhouse they ate dinner,
Stuffing themselves with two roast geese at least
And picking their teeth with thin bone from drumsticks
They slept that night on fatter featherticks,
Mother Holl shook down feathers from the sky.   50

A pail of time tipped back into another pail,
Leftover fly from summer buzzing on ceiling,
A feather gleamed upon Peter's wrist and Ann
Swept the top of the stove with a goosewing.

Drowning in the waterflames of Love
They lay in the straw with it snowing in the loft window.

Keziah quite an old goose gray as the winter twilight in a city
Clambered up into her nest to begin laying.
She was like
Coming out of the William Avenue Public Library,   60
People flowing up Main Street,* sadly,
Each person a gray feather, the streetlights like
All the possible eggs inside her and the streetcar an orange beak
coming toward you.

---

* Winnipeg

5

POEMS 1960–65

The Alphabet

Where are the fields of dew?
I cannot keep them.
They quip and pun
The rising sun
Who plucks them out of view:
But lay down fire-veined jasper!

For out of my cloudy head
Come Ay Ee I Oh and U,
Five thunders shouted;
    Drive in sardonyx!   10

And Ull Mm Nn Rr and hisSsings
Proclaim huge wings;
Pour in sea blue sapphires!

Through my bristling hair
Blows Wuh and Yuh
Puh, Buh, Phuh and Vuh,
The humorous air:
Lift up skies of chalcedony!

Huh, Cuh, Guh and Chuh
Grunt like pigs in my acorn mind: 20
Arrange these emeralds in a meadow!

Come down Tuh, Duh and Thuh!
Consonantly rain
On the windowpane
Of the shrunken house of the heart;
Lift up blood red sardius!

Lift up golden chrysolite!
Juh, Quuh, Zuh and X
Scribble heavens with light,
    Steeples take fright.   30

In my mouth like bread
Stands the shape of this glory;
Consonants and vowels
Repeat the story:
And sea-green beryl is carried up!

The candle tongue in my dark mouth
Is anguished with its sloth
And stung with self-scoff
As my eyes behold this treasure.
Let them bring up topaz now!   40

Dazzling chrysoprase!
Dewdrops tempt dark wick to sparkle.
Growl Spark! you whelp and cur,
Leap out of tongue kennel
And candle sepulchre.

I faint in the hyacinthine quarries!
My words pursue
Through the forest of time
The fading antlers of this dew.

A B C D E F G H I J K L M   50
Take captive the sun
Slay the dew quarry
Adam's Eve is morning rib
Bride and bridegroom marry
Still coffin is rocking crib
Tower and well are one
The stone is the wind, the wind is the stone
New Jerusalem
N O P Q R S T U V W X Y Z !

1960

To Bishop Berkeley

How beautiful the barnyard is,
    The little flashlight says.
Wherever I look is shining
    And active as plays.

So says the lamp within the house
    At golden plaster, golden walls
And candles remark how wainscot
    Gleams like calls.

Even the urinal match said,
    Oh what beautiful hands,   10
And the oozy willow-the-wisp
    Marvelled blue quicksands.

Oh Wordsworth and nature-walkers
    Thy nature barnyard is;
Her trees are plaster, wainscot hills,
    Handy vale and miry mess.

Wherever walks your lantern self
    The crop of wonder then sprouts up;
        Five kinds of music,
The spear of time, the spatial cup.   20

1961

The Butterfly and the Moth

The Earth, that huge & dirty Lout,
Has my five bonfires all put out.

See these two pebbles, they're my eyes.
My ears have changed to windy skies.
My tongue's become a dead snail shell
And brown leaves paste my sense of smell.
My instruments of pleasure are   20
The dead weeds' winter wind guitar.

With rotten sighs and whizzing sounds
I fade in a thousand burial grounds.

Alas, beneath the drifts of snow
No greens for caterpillars grow.
I'll build of nothing and of sorrow
From ashes and of autumn dust
A cradle coffin ark which must
Somehow float me to tomorrow.

In my dead hands grows a fine grass,   10
The waste fork sprouts a mushroom.
In my eyes come the Sun & the Moon.
I hear again the South Wind pass,
In my nails rise rain white clouds.
My empty head teems flower crowds,
And sing me to a Butterfly
Who wise & reckless passes by
The tight closed flowers of death and doth
Leave them for the brown winged moth.

1961

Near Tobermory, Ontario

I look upon a blue cove
     In August
With egg pebble beach,
Blue sky & cedar birch sides.

And I look upon the sisters four
     Blue sky & blue water
     Rock, pebble & earth
And the light I see it with.

Watty Blue has a drowned man
     For her heart   10
And rain for food & wind
To crisp her thoughts with.

Pale Blue Airy has clouds
To mind & winds to sing,
Thunder to say, lightning to do
     And birds to hold.

Urtha lumpily clogs
     Her clotty feet,
Waves Aaron's Rod & wears
     Emeralds in rags.   20

But Light, you're quite another thing.
     Indeterminate,
You hold them all yet let them slip
     Into themselves again.

1963

190

Starling with a Split Tongue

Some boys caught me
    In the yard
And with a jackknife they
Split my tongue into speech
So in a phrenological cage
Here in the garage I stay
    And say
The cracklewords passersby taught.
I say I know not what
Though I pray I do not pray   10
Though I curse I do not curse
Though I talk I do not talk

"I thought that made it kinda nice"
I heard her say as she began slipping on the ice
    The the I am   An a am I
    I and am are the & a   Who is are? Who saw war?
I rock a little pronoun   It does instead of me
I rose as I   Nooned as you
Lay down as he or she   Begat we, you & they
My eggs are covered with commas   20

    "Yuh remember when she fell down in a fit?"
    Reveries Jake from the bottom of the pit.

Before beforeday   after St. After's Massacre
While the while is on   Since since is since
Let's wait till till   Or until if you like
I come from from   to Whither Bay
Down Whence Road   but not To-day

As still as infinitives were the   Stones
Filled with adjectives were the   Trees
And with adverbs the   Pond   30
This all is a recorded announcement
                    This all is a recorded announcement
"I thought that made it kinda nice"
"Yuh remember . . . . in a fit?"
                              Darkness deep
Now fills the garage and its town
                              With wordless sleep.

Who split their tongues? I ask.
Of Giant Jackknife in the sky.
Who split their tongues into lie mask   40
And lie face; split their hand
Into this way, that way, up and down,
Divided their love into restless hemispheres,
Split into two — one seeing left, one right
Their once one Aldebaran all-seeing eye?
In the larger garage of the endless starlight
          Do they not croak as I?

1964

THE YOUNG TRAVELLER

i) Going for the Mail

After four, when home from school.
    A boy down the farm walks,
To get the mail the mailman's left
    In the backroad mailbox.

Oh things to watch and things to think
    As I walk down the lane
Between the elmtree and the fence
    Things that are not plain.

For instance is the elmtree there
    Still there when I am past it?   10
I jump about and there it is
    Certain to all my wit.

But could it still not be
    That when my back is turned
It disappears and nothing is?
    Why not, I've still not learned.

There's sedge in the marsh to look at
    And dark brown curled dock.
Why do I love the weeds so
    And examine every stalk?   20

Back at the house they tell him
    That although he was at the mailbox
He forgot to get the mail out
    So back again he walks.

    The fields are dark, the sky dark gray
    The farmhouse lights come on
And dimmer lights in barns,
    One reflected in the pond.

This time there's less to think upon
    Since all the detail's gone   30
But what news and what mail I get
    To reflect upon –

The world in huge butterflies of paper –
    (And here's the comfort)
Will still not be as interesting
    As walking twice for it.

ii) To School

Of chips for the fire a boxful
    Gathered quickly in the yard
And then off I run –
    Across the fields to school.

I run on my own path that I've made
    Like a smaller sort of cow.
The meadow's past and now the bush
    Where at night you'd be afraid.

Sunny hollow with violet,
    Wise old elmtree tall;   10
My path fades out in the marshy flats
    Where you often get your feet wet.

The frogs are singing here and there
    A scarlet tanager flies off,
Off into the dark green bush.
Here's the spring that gurgles a crystal air!

"Out of a rusty pipe I flow.
    I fall in a silver string.
Cup your hands and drink of me
    The child of rain and snow.   20

You are the child of sun and man
    And to your school you go
To learn of numbers and letters there.
    But wiser and prettier than

My cool clear quench you'll never learn
    At that school or any other.
So learn it now and drink of me
    Before to school you turn . . ."

There's the school and its yard
    Filled with ball or crack the whip.   30
Near the apple tree I hear the bell
    And I run now very hard.

At school when I sharpen my pencil
    I look back across to home:
Meadow bush marsh spring fence tree –
    Of Heaven the windowsill.

iii) To Sunday School

The school on Sundays is a Sunday School
And so the way to it's the same
Except that Sunday morning air is golden
And each summer Sunday thing a slow burning jewel.

Father and Mother do not run, nor do I
Because with Timothy and sweet clover,
A tangled bee buzzing yellow green forest,
The meadow's grown tumbly and head high.

The summer shade of trees is solid black
And where my path appears again   10
The pasture grass has gone to seed
And thoughtful cows look stolid back.

In the marshy flats the weeds are rank,
Curled Dock brown and Cut Grass scrapy,
Lady's Thumb and the green knitting needles
Of Club Rush along the dry ditch bank.

Here is Cousin Tommy's field of peas,
Fifteen acres of cool green involved
Succulence; were it not that we'd break
Several commandments we'd stay and eat at our ease.   20

The school yard's dead still in the sun,
The window panes buzz with Doxology.
We're late and just at the very last fence,
But only walk quickly – not run.

Oh Sunday walk of plants and animals!
From thy green fars and golden nearnesses
I've learnt already the Sunday School lesson:
That Earth may lie within Heaven's walls.

iv) The Stoneboat

What is a stoneboat you want to know?
A stoneboat is a wooden sleigh
That bumping glides over grass or loam
And does not need the snow.

195

In that plowed field over there
    We're told to pick up the stones.
To the stoneboat lying in the yard
    We hitch up the blind mare.

From its weed entangled rest
    She lurches out the stoneboat   10
From underneath a mouse streaks out
    And we see its brown grass nest.

In the nest are little pink things
    At least a dozen of them,
A blind soft rose in the dry brown nest
    Of faint movings and squeakings.

On no wheels, on only itself
    The wooden boat glides on.
Down the cowpath lane stream
    Like a square wooden swan.   20

To the brown ocean field where float
    The mysterious scattered stones:
Pink, blue, speckled and gray
    We tote them onto the stone boat.

What are you, speckled egg-shaped stone?
    You cannot speak, you cannot see
    You cannot hear, but can you think?
For you seem blessed with a life of your own.

In the gray sky fades the sun.
    We turn back to the yard   30
With a cargo of stones each different
    We unhitch and our job is done.

Their mother has carried the pink mice away.
    The blind mare eats her supper grass.
The blind stones dream on the curious ship
    And the blind world waits for the day.

v) The Cutter

The farm lies drowned in snow.
In the yard Bob barks at the sparrows.
Our elders hitch the cutter up
            And off we go.

My cousin and I sit facing our mothers.
    The barn and Bob and House grow smaller
If we were to turn round we'd see
    Things approaching us grow taller.

Tring tring tring the cutter bells ring.
    We count passing hydro poles   10
In whose forlorn and gray fiddle wires
    The five cold north winds sing.

Bushes in the ditch on our left hand.
    Red bramble canes in the white snow,
Red hips on the gray thorn bushes
    White white field on our right hand.

White white white white white white
    Tring tring tring tring tring tring
Low in the sky the December sun
    Seen through branches as black as night.   20

(Smaller and smaller grow the house and Bob)
    Now thick fir trees block off the wind.
We suddenly hear what our mothers are saying
    And the wind in the dark trees hushedly sob.

Then past us the great ash tree glides
    Wearing an armour of icy glare
And down down down down the hill we fall
    As the cutter to the river bridge slides.

We ride in a voyageur's boat, not a cutter,
Down the white waterfall. We crouch   30
On the back of a bird not a boat,
A wooden belled soaring bird hur -

Rying, not a bird but an angel
    Covered with bells gliding down
From the stars and the clouds
    Great news and glad tidings to tell.

In grandfather's kitchen our harbor at last
    We thaw ourselves out at the stove.
I close my eyes, still we glide, still we shoot!
    Sailors of the White Sea and birds of the Blast!   40

vi) The Buggy

Four red wheels the buggy rolls
Down the lane beside the hydro poles.

Quickly it rattles, quickly it goes
Down the soft brown lane by the wild rose -

Bush and catches in the blur of its spokes
Heads of blue chicory and Queen Anne's folks.

The apple tree branchily brushes its hood,
We crunch onto gravel at the beekeeper's wood.

Between two poplar trees wind tossing
And over the wild strawberry railway crossing   10

And in between fences grown thick with wild plum
And hawthorns matted with creamy blossom.

At Brock's place the guinea fowls cry "Robbers!"
And a boy is milking a goat who eats burs.

Much more the four red wheels will bring us
Will rail fences, barking dogs, rivers sing us.

Clouds sun blue sky dark green forest
Whose cool shade slows us almost to rest.

Clouds moon shooting stars secret lake low
To all these wonders the buggy will go   20

Four red wheels through the nights and the days,
Queen of the spring, the summer and the fall ways.

vii) The Car

Our hired man was also our mailman.
One Saturday morning
In early spring
He took me on his route in his Model A sedan.

First there was the dim letter sorting Post Office
And all the other mail men
Filling up their bags and then
Out we set on the wet streets black as licorice.

Then we drove till we were out of town
And the rain wind filled   10
The crackled windshield
With fringes of rain pearls dribbling down.

Ahead of us stretched Rural Route Four
Two hundred mailboxes on posts
Like helmeted Roman military ghosts
And we with some mail for each headpiece they wore.

Here's the farm of Farmer Sloat.
One letter with a red stamp
One newspaper slightly damp
We put in his box's gray weathered iron throat.   20

Chugg chuggity sputter sputter rattle
Splashing through puddles
Slowing down in muddles
The old car moves with its cargo of tattle.

Letters for some and nothing for others
Blazing seed catalogues
Political demagogues
Babies' golliwogs
Family Herald and *Weekly Star*
Gurgly remedies for catarrh   30
Birthday cookies (somewhat crunched) from grandmothers -

Etcetera Etcetera etcetera etcetera.
Green fields and blue distance
Stopped, then slid by in clumsy dance,
Then stopped again still as a camera.

The car now is empty, the sky's turned blue
We've brought the world to all of you,
On Rural Route Four to everyone
And we see as we look at the fresh yellow sun
The clouds have sown their letters too.   40

viii) The Train

In the early dawn world of no colours
We drive through a still sleeping town.
The streetlamps are tired of their nightwatch.
The train has not yet come down.

The ground shakes. Roar! And here it comes!
Close up blows its hair raising cry.
Like a whale it spouts steam, like a lighthouse
It flashes its one bright and powerful eye.

Slowly the train starts to move. "All Aboard!"
Cries the gold buttoned man who took us   10
In hand when we climbed on the train.
By the gaslight we see such a ruckus

For somebody's sat on a sleepy man's hat.
As the train moves so slowly at first
We see waving parents and the outskirts of town
And then faster come bushes and fields in a burst

Of more and more thundering hammering speed.
There's the farm, our house and the elm tree tall.
The windows are gold with the sun getting up.
Even now they grow smaller and small –   20

Er and vanish! The train with its crossing cries
Has great round giant feet
And a mile long rush of black hair. It can
Diminish great forests, make still stones fleet:

Swing fences back like crack-the-whip,
Pull whole towns in a minute closer,
Blur thousands of daisies into one big daizzz –
Leaving things smaller, coming things grosser.

It beats on the bridges like hollow drums,
It flows the telegraph wires beside,   30
It waves kids at us, chases cows away,
Parts trees to reveal what hills will hide.

Till it brings us, at last to stillness and stop
Yes, with all its thunder and pronto
(I wonder how small our home house is now?)
It brings us to Aunt's house in Toronto.

Yes, Train, how small is our house back there now?
We've been brought so fast and so far
I should guess that it's smaller than thought
      Or grains of poppy seed are.   40

1964

200

Eight Christmas Cards

Matthew tells of Christ's begetters
They are known as Jesse's stem
From this tree of old ancestors
    Came God's son

This tree still stands along the fence
A gnarled lopped maple tree
Each twig and branch a prince
Pointing to glory

Glory over the winter fields
    Child of David and Solomon
Glory over the fields of snow
    Point tree to the sun

1958

        * * *

    Wisdom and simplicity
Crowns and shepherds' crooks
    Come to Bethlehem to see
How a baby God looks

1959

        * * *

Beside the road the snow fence stands
And holds the snow in slatty hands.
Once our humanity did hold
A dove of white, a boy of gold.

1960

A :   . AA'
ᵇV ᵥ A;   :A ⅀₄EEF'
 'TSCI Ǝ H: : ;O O ONn
;EBAgI ⅁Iꟼ ;   . O ·ᐺᐺᐺᐺʇ :
 ɟ u EXV ƕʇ :   ; ᑫ ʃ ˙sus grryᴡɒyʋ;
'DT TUVMⱫℓ7   ɟ   ɩBET   ɩHUISɩ
ɩ Qɑɐs ɩ   ᑫLINꟻESV ɩ   ɩ''k   ᑫdSYⱫ⅀ ꬵʌɯɩ
   no oooooꟽWTⱫ ɩ : Υ ɩ N WΛ⊥o ooooot
ᴚʋq   o o ooo   ɩ l ɩ   .   A o   o ɩ
i   o   o   w ⅄⅄ ɩ⅄⅄ ɩ   ɩ ɩʃx   o   ?
ʇɑ ʋ zᴜᴜ ʋʋ Xr ɩ⅄!   ⅄⅄ⱼᵢ lll ɪ!!   ᵣXg g ʃd ''., ɪɯ ɩ
ɩɩɩɩɩɩ ɩɩɩɩɩɩrɩɩɩɩɩɩɩɩɩɩɩɩɩɩɩ ɩɩɩɩ.ɩ!.ɩ:ɩ ɩ O   ɩɩɩɩɩɩɩjɩɩɩɩɩɩɩɩɩɩ:ɩɩ.ɩ.ɩɩɩɩɩɩɩ ɩɩɩɩɩɩ⅄⅄
  ꭈꭈ ꭈ ꭈ ꭈ⊤o ꭈ ꭈꭈ ꭈꭈꭈ⁊⁊'''`''''lll,ꟼllllᴜʋ''''`'ꭈ ꭈ ꭈꭈ ꭈ ꭈ ꭈ ꭈ ... ꬵɩ ɩ
  ɛɛɛɛɛɛɛɛɛɛᴐ ɛ ɛꭗɛᴐ·ɩɛᴐɛᴐɛᴐᴐᴐᴐᴐᴐᴐᴐᴐᴐᴐ·⅄IHSᴐᴐɛᴐᴐᴐᴐᴐᴐᴐᴐᴐᴐᴐᴐᴐᴐᴐᴐᴐᴐᴐᴐᴐ·ᴐᴐᴐ ɛɛ
  ɛ AXꜱ ᴎ⅃ ɛɛ ɩ ɛxꜱᴐ ʲɛ G   ɛ , ꜱu x ꜱ ɛ ʲ ʲzᵉ? ɛ ?ᵉ
   ɛ ʃ ꜱgʃ A   ꜱꜱ   ꜱ   N   ɛ ᴘᴘ ᴘ   Zꜱ i d g ɛ
   ɛ ꜱ ɛⱿ Ð   ɛ   ⅀   ɛ   ᴐ ᴐ ꜱᴜ ɛ
   ●DEO D   ᴐ   Ꝁ   ɛ   SUTTANPᴅ ɛ
     ᴐ   ꟼᴐᴈ   ᴐ   O   ᴐ   ᴐɘʇ ꟼɐxᴐ
     ʇ. ꭈ ɩ   ɩ   ɪi   i   !
   ⅄⅄ᴙⱭⱭᴙ⅃Ɑ⅄⅄   ?   Kꭍ⅄⅄⅀⅄⅄⅃!!
   Kꟼ⅄KⱭⱭⱭⱭⱭN   ꟽ ꟽ ꟽ ꟽ ꟽ
   ICH₄ᴐꟻHᴐG   GHHCꟻꟻEEI
   ꬵꬵꬵꬵꬵꭍ   ꬵꬵꬵꬵꬵꬵ ꬵꭍꬰ
   ꭍ   ꭍ

From Time's cocoon
And the caterpillar of prophecy
Comes to Bethlehem
A shining laughing baby butterfly.

This butterfly is Christ whom we
Since He is the Word made flesh
Do fashion verbally.

1961

This golden key was found today
Within a manger filled with hay
Run with it to our prison door
The stalls of death hold us no more

1962

* * *

Crystallography
Determines what You are:
On the wind's dark sleeve
My Shepherd's Star.

1963

* * *

Of Heaven's love
This endless knot
At Bethlehem
Our string of time
In a cradle caught

1964

* * *

On his birthday there is a blue sky
In the swale there's clear ice
Two boys skate an X, the Greek letter Chi
Because it stands for Christ

1965

203

Gifts

Existence gives to me
What does he give to thee?

He gives to me :   a pebble
He gives to me :   a dewdrop
He gives to me :   a piece of string
He gives to me :   a straw

Pebble   dewdrop   piece of string   straw

The pebble is a huge dark hill I must climb
The dewdrop's a great storm lake you must cross
The string was a road he could not find   10
The straw will be a sign whose meaning they forget

Hill   lake   road   sign

What was it that quite changed the scene
So desert fades into meadows green?

The answer is that they met a Tiger
The answer is that he met a Balloon,
A Prostitute of Snow, a Gorgeous Salesman
As well as a company of others such as
Sly Tod, Reverend Jones, Kitty Cradle and so on

Who was the Tiger?   Christ   20
Who was the Balloon?   Buddha
Emily Brontë and the Emperor Solomon
Who sang of his foot in the doorway.
All these met him. They were hopeful and faithful.

Now the mountain becomes   a pebble in my hand
The lake calms down   to a dewdrop in a flower
The weary road   is a string around your wrist
The mysterious sign   is a straw that whistles "Home"

Pebble   dewdrop   piece of string   straw

1965

The Killdeer

There was nothing left but the killdeer.
    He skated the cold spring air
Over the old pasture, the line of elms,
    The Easter farmhouse, I there

        Heard him cry:
There lived a man by Spiral Lake
    And he my grandfather was;
Seven children did he make
    And this is what their names were:

Mars and Mercury were two little boys,   10
    Luna and Venus the girls:
Jupiter and Saturn had moons for toys
    And their brother Sun for light, sir.

In my grandfather's spacious garden groin
    His tree of children grew,
And grandchild I in my earthy nest
    There first sung and flew.

I went to school with Milky Way;
    She was the daughter of Spiral Lake,
Oh little Milky, temporal and speckled,   20
    Cow-pocked, milk-splashed and gay.

But the farm-nest tipped
    And Father split in two;
Uncle Good and Aunt Evil
    Took me in, how do you do.

They lived in a House of Day
    It had a Yard of Night;
It stood on a street of Puzzle Town
    On a refuse graveyard site.

Behind the gasworks Cain got me.   *30*
    He crushed me like a nettle.
A sweet faced boy named Abel brought me
    His dearest treasure, a piece of gravel.

After he died his brother Seth
    Spat out the apple-pip
And said with magic breath;
    Come out of this Puzzle Town.

Where shall we go? I said.
    Outside the city limits
Lie the farms of dread   *40*
    Stocked with fear herds and bite crops.

There's a lake—we'll swim in it,
    Said Seth with a flourish.
There's a tree, we'll sit under it.
    He blew a trumpet.

Now the lake was Milky Way's
    Underpettiwhirlyworld,
And the tree, so my friend says,
    Was Grandfather's old cane.

Then up sprang Uncle and Aunt Good and Evil.   *50*
    They came out at us screaming:
Stop that fornicating
    In the bushes with that milkywaymaid.

We see no wrong, did we sing back,
    No rampant rogues, no slut,
Nothing but
Time crossing space, planet tree and milky lake.

The tree looked at itself in the water,
  We bent it down in the milky depth;
    A seven-oared boat   60
Discovered the elusive daughter.

We sang out with crucified jewsharps.
  Aunt and Uncle turned into gate posts,
We sang in wooden flats and naily sharps,
  The Yard went into the House.

Seth said: "Swallow the stone he gave you!"
  I did and behold these marvellous things:
Abel flew by like a mile high killdeer
    With six wings.

Cain turned into his thistly nest,   70
  Puzzle Town solved itself,
The Farm tipped back at last
  And my Father mended.

A sky of cloudy breasts
  Rained milk:
The blood of a giant heart
  Pounded beneath my crystal raft.

There was nothing left but the killdeer,
  He skated the cold spring air
Over the old pasture, the line of elms,   80
  The Easter farmhouse, I there

    Heard his cry
And saw all vanish into him:
All time, all Space, all Bible
  Into that giant stormy die.

1965

6 TWELVE LETTERS TO A SMALL TOWN - 1962

■ FIRST LETTER

To the Avon River above Stratford, Canada

What did the Indians call you?
For you do not flow
With English accents.
I hardly know
What I should call you
    Because before
I drank coffee or tea
    I drank you
    With my cupped hands
And you did not taste English to me   10
    And you do not sound
    Like Avon
    Or swans & bards
But rather like the sad wild fowl
    In prints drawn
    By Audubon
And like dear bad poets
    Who wrote
    Early in Canada
And never were of note.   20
You are the first river
    I crossed
And like the first whirlwind
    The first rainbow
    First snow, first
    Falling star I saw,
You, for other rivers are my law.
    These other rivers:
    The Red & the Thames
    Are never so sweet   30
To skate upon, swim in
    Or for baptism of sin.
    Silver and light

The sentence of your voice,
    With a soprano
Continuous cry you shall
    Always flow
    Through my heart.
The rain and the snow of my mind
Shall supply the spring of that river   40
    Forever.
Though not your name
Your coat of arms I know
    And motto:
A shield of reeds and cresses
    Sedges, crayfishes
The hermaphroditic leech
Minnows, muskrats and farmers' geese
And printed above this shield
One of my earliest wishes   50
"To flow like you."

◾ *SECOND LETTER*

Instructions: How to Make a Model of the Town

A First take two sticks and two leafy branches.
B First take two sticks and two leafy branches.
A Put their ends together so they form spokes.
B Put their ends together so they form spokes.
A The spokes of an invisible wheel.
B Coming together at the centre and fanning out?
A Coming together at the centre and fanning out—
   These sticks and branches are
   The principal through streets of the town.
B Huron Street and Ontario Street can be leafy branch streets. 10
A Downie and Erie can be the bare stick streets.

B Now, what will we do with these glass bubbles?
A Put the three blue ones at the end of
    The three Great Lakes streets — Erie Street,
B Ontario Street and Huron Street.
A They eventually reach those lakes but
    Hang the green glass ball at the end of Downie Street
    Because it fades into farms and fields and townships.
B I can't think what we're going to make the houses of.
A We'll make model houses out of berries.   20
    Take some berries. Ripe gooseberries for red houses.
    White raspberries for yellow brick houses.
B White raspberries for yellow brick houses.
A Sprinkle white and red currants, cherries,
    And trees can be represented by their leaves.
B And trees can be represented by their leaves.
    One elm leaf for a whole elm tree,
    And streets laid out with rows of berry houses.
A From the air, you know, a small town
    Must look like rows of berries in the grass.   30
    Now take some red apples and some russet apples,
    Put these along the main streets for the business places.
    Three potatoes each for the Court House
    St. Joseph's Church (R.C.) and St. James's (C. of E.).
B Three potatoes each for the Court House,
    St. Joseph's Church (R.C.) and St. James's (C. of E.).
A Buildings around Market Square—ditto.
B Buildings around Market Square—ditto.
A With a rather sharpside brick-coloured tomato in the centre of the
      Market Square—to stand for the three towered City Hall.
B What'll we do to represent the people?   40
A Well we could dress up lady bugs.
B But it's a hot July day and I hear a band.
    Please, couldn't we finish this later
    And see the band now?
A Fall down then! Fall down!
    Into our model of the town.
B Hey! Look at all those bugs
    Lady and gentleman bugs!
A Regard the carved potato Court House
    And observe the firm tomato City Hall.   50
B And streets like branches and boughs
    Hung with the orchards and pears of
    Houses, houses, people, houses, houses.
A Fall down! Fall down!
    Into our model of the town!

213

✶ THIRD LETTER

Orange Lilies

On the twelfth day of July
King William will ride by
        On a white horse
        On a white charger
King William And Queen Mary
    He bears an orange lily
        In his hand
        (He in front
        And she behind,
        On a white horse   10
        On a white charger)
    And so does she
On a white horse.

    They're riding to see
    And to jump the Boyne
        With a white horse
        In their groin

On the twelfth day of July
King William will ride by
    With a white horse   20
King William with Queen Mary.

✱ FOURTH LETTER

Voices and Prepositions

Up here is the Water Tower, down there's the Sewage Farm
Down there's the Old Folks' Home, up here's the Theatre
Up here's a pillared house, down there is Kent Lane

    The roof of a small brewery by moonlight
Up here's the Hospital and across here is the graveyard
Up the Stone Bridge, along the Dam, into the Churches,
Across the Market Square and on the Crimean cannon

    Sunlight on a two-headed eagle
Through the market with Amish bonnets and beards,   10
Eggs and gladiolis, sausages and cooked cheese
An old negro with a lump on the back of his neck
Sitting forever in the silent Saturday summer sun

    In the door of the livery stable
A girl with a branch of lilac in her hand
Walking down summer Wellington Street
A white Sunday factory in the waste outskirts
Like a monastery: lonely, empty, austere

    A girl with no hair playing by the dam
Huge gold paper bells swinging over Northway's store   20
  Recorded ding dongs from a loudspeaker
A hundred gold paper Christmas tree angels
  In Kresge's dime store just after the war.

■ FIFTH LETTER

The Cloakroom at the High School

The high school is the palace of Merlin and Cheiron
  Where governors and governesses teach
The young Achilles and young Arthurs of the town.

The radiators teach the rule of monotony
  Cheep cheep cheeping in the winter classroom
Timid fingers learn to turn a fire on.

A stuffed hummingbird and a stuffed sandhill crane.
  In the dusty looking glass of grammar,
Number, the young see the shape of their brain.

But what and where did I learn most from?   10
High, dark, narrow as its single window
In the old high school there was a cloakroom—

A cloakroom! In winter stuffed with cloaks
  Soft with outside things inside
Burs, mud, dead leaves on some of the coats.

At four o'clock there are forty-nine bare hooks
  As a hundred hands reach up
And I, lingering rearranging my books

See sweeping face peer in of janitor
  Alone in the winter twilight
The old janitor! An image to ponder over.   20

Of course I learnt snow dripping windows
  Corridors of words, cobwebs of character,
The ninety-two elements in a long row,
        But most I learnt

The insoluble mystery of the cloakroom
  And the curious question of the janitor
    In some way so centre and core
      January man and cloakroom
From which the moon each month unlocks upon the wave
  A white bird.   *30*

✱ *SIXTH LETTER*

A House on King William Street

    Like the life here
The wallpaper repeats itself
  Up and down go the roses
  Similar blows struck out
By air-banging green fists:
A bright rose and a blue one
A pink blow and a blue one

The years have not changed their likeness
    Except that those behind the sofa
    Have kept their original blaze   *10*
    And these opposite the window
      Have turned yellow.

    Aunt Henny says to Aunt Penny,
"Have you read *She?* Oh a terrible book,
  An awful book! Yes, it's by
    Haggard Rider Haggard."

    Aunt Lurkey says to Aunt Turkey:
"I nearly slipped today, I nearly
    Slipped today.
  We should put a piece of carpet   *20*
    On that particular step
      We should,"
Says Aunt Lurkey taking another should
    Off the would pile.

    No one remembers when
  The wallpaper was new, except
    The wallpaper itself
In the green smothered darkness behind
    The sofa and the cupboard.

And I, I their awkward fool   *30*
Board there while I go to school.

✱SEVENTH LETTER

Prose for the Past

What was it like in the past?

Find out in the archives of the Public Library. In a small cellar room, there they keep the tea coloured files of the town's newspapers. A shaky fading paper rope into the darkness of the past some more than a century long. You open the door with a skeleton key—the door, has it a white china doorknob? And there in the dark little room, the summer sunlight smothered by a frayed yellow drawn down window blind—there is the past.

Long ago Stratford was a small little embryonic amoeba of a place. Things were paid for in pounds and shillings. The price of grain and cordwood would go up in the winter and down in the summer, as I remember. Each fall there was a list of the crimes to be tried at the Assizes—respectable crimes too. People—I remember a Swiss traveller —stabbed in a tavern. There were fairs at which young men rode at the ring, bears ran away with little boys and ate them up, Indians stole an ancestor's clothing while he was in swimming, flax was grown in huge quantities and it was laid out to ret on land east of the city which still looks as if it had been used for some peculiarly damp purpose. Two boys, David and Jonathan, drowned in the river.

When the Crimean War comes someone writes a poem that starts Hail Britannia, Hail Terrific Gal. Next Week we are informed that he didn't mean Gal, he meant Hail Terrific Gaul. Haha.

As we read the weekly paper then one can't help noticing how winter affects the little place. Nothing happens except cordwood is consumed in stoves and there are stage coaches and toll gates but still — what is happening is snow. Then in the spring the heart begins to beat more quickly again and there are actually more words in the paper.

218

The railway attempts to come to town, sinks down in a very powerful slough, causeways itself out and changes things. Gaslight and train whistles and running trees, moons and clouds. I can hear all the wheels of the past—grinding, singing, creaking, whirling in a fountain of sound at the place where the four branches meet and there have been footsteps and voices without stop now for more than a century. Cutters and sleds dashing and jingling like elegant wooden fish this way and that. Then the flower or is it a seed pod of all the words spoken at the cross-roads of the town, the footsteps stopped and the wheels turned, bursts open into figures from the deep past I didn't have to read about for we heard of them from ancestral voices or saw them just the once with one's own eyes.

There was the Indian woman who worked at pulling flax and drank vinegar.

In the past people showed what they thought of themselves much more openly than they do now. You saw very very happy people striding down the street with their hands clasped behind their backs. You saw very very proud people—a doctor's wife say, of high degree, walking down Wellington Street with their noses literally in the air and their eyes proudly averted.

There was an old blind fiddler who always played at the gate of the Fair Grounds and people put pennies in his violin case.

There were the old ladies who stopped the church bells from ringing after midnight because it disturbed their slumbers.

An Indian crossing the Market Square in the November twilight with a long feather in his hat.

There was an old woman called Granny Crack who every child has heard about who wore seven dresses all at once and walked the length and breadth of the country begging for a living, trading and begging. She speaks from the past:

> I was a leather skinned harridan
> I wandered the country's roads
> Trading and begging and fighting
> With the sun for hat and the road for shoes.
>
> You saw me freckled and spotted
> My face like a bird's egg
> When, berry picking kids, you ran from me
> Frightened, down the lane by the wood.

They saw her as an incredible crone
The spirit of neglected fence corners
Of the curious wisdom of brambles
And weeds, of ruts, of stumps and of things despised.
I was the mother of your sun
I was the aunt of your moon
My veins are your paths and roads
On my head I bear steeples and turrets
I am the darling of your god.

The old woman of the country, Summer Wanderer,
The old man of the town, Winter Janitor,
   Old Women, Granny Crack
   Old man, old woman
       Revolving back to back
          Looking down
            Granny Janitor Angel
             On my town.

* EIGHTH LETTER

The Music Lesson

In the old fantastic house which one remembers as having huge green
elm trees, red velvet curtains, tied back with pink and gold butterflies
(but I add this from my Great Aunt Mary's front parlour) marble
fireplaces like Roquefort Cheese and much carved chairs, clock under
glass bell, a steel engraving of John Knox with calves on his legs so huge
they might be Bibles he was smuggling past the border in his stockings;
so strange—at my music teacher's house at the back there was a
railway track with trains going by. In dreams the engine of the train
always stands still and starts one off on the scales with a big blast on
the steam whistle.

After waiting in the hallway with the Fathers of Confederation, the
History of the Dutch Republic, pictures of Greek Statues interestingly
disfigured and De la Motte Fouqué's *Ondine* gorgeously illustrated by
Edmund Dulac—after that—the Lesson.

Teacher Now I'll set the metronome
  Pupil I am very far from home
Teacher We have half an hour to play
  Pupil In an auditory way
Teacher Play us your scales first in the form of our town's
        streets

220

Pupil	A Baptist minister walking up Nile Street
	An Arabian girl running down Douglas Street
	A French teacher on Wellington Street
	A Sunday School teacher on St. Patrick's Street
	A truant officer on Romeo Street
	An uppity type on Downie Street
	A Welshman on Britannia Street
	An Irishman on Caledonia Street
Teacher	Now play me some grocers and store keepers.
Pupil	There was a grocer who had a sad little store
	He wore straw cuffs at his wrists.

There was a seedsman whose name was Seed
Fat as a well fed daffodil bulb.

There were twin grocers. Mr. Esau
And Mr. Jacob, white aproned in dimness,
Selling rare First Editions of Kellogg's Cornflakes.

There was my Great Aunt Mary
Who ran the Britannia Grocery
And was held up for what she had in the till
By an Indian. . . . Five bucks.

There were a brother and sister who ran
A bakery: their name was Bread
Miss Bread and Mr. Bread.

There was old Mrs. Mallard-Duck
She kept a Second Hand Store crammed with
The clocks and chairs and dishes of the past
And five children . . . grand . . . around the store.
Creaking rusty-voiced old Mrs. Mallard-Duck.

Teacher	That will do now. Now play me your pieces.
	Play me *The Storm*. What shall I set the metronome at?
Pupil	Set at summer and pink and white and yellow brick
	sunlight with blue sky and white feather dumpling
	clouds.

The Storm

          A cloud and a cloud and a cloudy
          Came into the blue afternoon room
          A cloud and a cloud and a cloud
                And a cloud and a cloud a cloud
                    Mac Leod
                      A Cloud
          And a Cloud and a cloudy

          Down down down came the cloudy
          With a windowpane shudder
          And mirrors for your feet
          People running into stores
          Darkness in the library
          Umbrellas blossom
          Church is nearer through the rain

          A cloud and a cloud and a cloudy
          Came out of the yellow garage.
          Joseph MacLeod in a many-coloured vest
          Danced to the Music dying in the west.

Teacher   Yes, you've both hands together very nicely on that.
              Up the tempo now and do keep practising your
              Snow Scenes and Interiors, your Skylines and City
              Limits. Let's have the next piece.
Pupil   Two Part Invention: a Year in the Town
Teacher   And how fast can you play it?
Pupil   Not very fast.
Teacher   Then you'd better play it hands separately.
              Left hand first.
Pupil   Bud bud budling
          Bud bud budling
          Bud bud budling
          Bud bud budling
              Buddy blossom
              Blossom buddies
              Budding blossoms
Teacher   The right hand for that:
Pupil   The spring winds up the town
          The spring winds up the town
Teacher   Left hand now:
          Leafy leafy leafy leafy
          Leaf Leaf Leaf Leaf
          Leafy leafy leafy leafy
          Leaf Leaf Leaf Leaf

<pre>
                  Leaves Leaves Leaves Leaves
                  Leaving leaves leaving leaves
                  Leafy leafy leaf leaf
Teacher   Right hand:
   Pupil   Frogs stop: Put out the glass wind lantern
                  Tinkling summer on the porch
              Frogs stop: Put out the glass wind lantern
                  Tinkling summer on the porch.
Teacher   Left hand.
   Pupil   Twig and branch, twig and branch
Teacher   Faster!
   Pupil   Twig and branch, twig and branch
              Bricks, stones and traffic hum
           Twig and branch, twig and branch
              Bricks, stones and traffic hum
           Twig and branch, twig and branch
              Bricks, stones and highway hum
              Bricks, stones and far away
           Twig and branch, branch and twig.
Teacher   The right hand for that now:
   Pupil   Crickets cry and the owl flies down.
           The ferris wheel and the fall rains fall
           Crickets cry and the owl flies down
           The ferris wheel and the fall rains fall.
Teacher   And let's hear the Left hand for Winter.
   Pupil   Blue and white, white and blue
              Orion rules the frosty town
           Blue and white, white and blue
              Orion rules the frosty town
           Blue and white, white and blue
              Orion rules the frosty town
           Blue and white, white and blue
              Orion rules the frosty town
           For three days no train or car got into town.
           The bakers had their yeast dropped from an airplane.
Teacher   Now! Hands together and not too fast, not too slow.
   Pupil Spring!
Bud bud budling
Bud bud budling   The spring winds up the town
Bud bud budling
Bud bud budling
Buddy blossom   The spring winds up the town
Blossom buddies
Budding blossoms
</pre>

223

Teacher Summer!
  Pupil

Leafy leafy leafy leafy   Frogs stop: put out
  Leaf leaf leaf leaf   the glass wind
Leafy leafy leafy leafy   lantern Tinkling
  Leaf leaf leaf leaf   summer on the
                                  porch.

Leaves leaves leaves leaves   Frogs stop: put out
  Leafy leafy leafy leafy   the glass wind
Leaving leaves leaving leaves   lantern Tinkling
  Leafy leafy leaf leaf   summer on the
                                  porch.

  Teacher Fall!
   Pupil

Twig and branch, twig and branch
  Bricks stones and traffic hum   Crickets cry
Twig and branch, twig and branch   and the owl
  Bricks stones and traffic hum   flies down
Twig and branch, twig and branch The ferris
  Bricks stones and highway hum   wheel and
  Bricks and stones and far away   the fall rains
Twig and branch, branch and twig fall
  Teacher Winter!
   Pupil

Blue and white, white and blue
  Orion rules the frosty town   For three days no
Blue and white, white and blue   train or car got
  Orion rules the frosty town   into the town.
Blue and white, white and blue The bakers had
  Orion rules the frosty town   their yeast
Blue and white, white and blue   dropped from
  Orion rules the frosty town   an airplane.
  Teacher Twice as fast next time.

✱ NINTH LETTER

Town House & Country Mouse

Old maids are the houses in town
They sit on streets like cement canals
  They are named after aldermen
    And their wives
  Or battles and dukes.

At a sky scratched with wires and smoke
They point their mild and weak gothic bonnets.
The houses of Albert and Brunswick Streets
Wait for farmers' barns to wed them
 But the streets are too narrow   10
  And they never come.

Out here barn is wedded to house,
 House is married to barn,
 Gray board and pink brick.
  The cowyard lies between
Where in winter on brown thin ice
  Red capped children skate.
 There is wallpaper in the house
   And in the barn
They are sawing the horns off a bull.   20

Out here the sound of bells on a wet evening
 Floating out clear when the wind is right.
 The factory whistles at noon in summer.
  Going from here to there
 As a child, not to a place with a name
  But first to get there:
The red buggy wheels move so fast
  They stand still
Whirling against sheaves of blue chicory
The secret place where wild bees nest   30
The million leaning pens of grass with their nibs of seed,
  The wild rose bush—all
   Suddenly gone.
On gravel now where corduroy logs from the past
   Look dumbly up
Buried in the congregations of gravel,
  Getting closer the highway
  Cars darting back and forth
  In another world altogether.
Past the stonemason's house with its cement lion 40
 Not something to be very much afraid of
  Since it has legs like a table,
 Past the ten huge willows, the four poplars.
  Far away in a field the slaughterhouse,
  Two gas stations with windy signs,
The half world of the city outskirts: orchards
 Gone wild and drowned farms.
  Suddenly the square:—

People turning and shining like lighted jewels,
  Terrifying sights: one's first nun!   50
    The first person with a wooden leg,
  A huge chimney writing the sky
      With dark smoke.
         A parrot.
A clock in the shape of a man with its face
      In his belly
        The swan
A Dixie cup of ice cream with a wooden spoon

And then—backwards, the gas stations,
  The outskirts, orchards, slaughterhouse   60
  Far back the chimneys still writing
    Four poplars, ten huge willows
    The lion with table legs.
The bump as we go over old corduroy log
The gamut of grass and blue flowers
    Until the wheels stop
    And we are not uptown
      We are here
Where barn is wedded to house . . .
    Into town, out of town.   70

Voices and Conjunctions

Who was the old man with two canes and a white beard
  Who walked along the road out of town
  With a huge sack on his back
    Who was that old man?

Mr. Vermeer, the specialist in trusses and supports,
  Lived in a sorrowful red brick house
Black ribbons on his pince-nez, black Homburg hat,
  Who had two grave bespectacled kids
    Eighty years old at the age of eight.

The old bookbinder who lived above the creamery   10
Huge butter churns walloped just under our feet
Had a gold and blue sign: printed wedding invitations
    Who had bound books in 1890 in Philadelphia.

There were remarkable boys on the streets
One who looked sad because his face was
Covered with whelks; he delivered papers
With a wagon; also an evil red-haired boy
Delivered groceries, said something I didn't hear
    Which made the girl in the store cry.

Gospel mad man who preached on the streets.   20
      Every day was like Sunday.
Far off you could hear him at school
    Who was like a big buzzing Bible bee.

Two brick tile kilns at the edge of town
      Two huge mosaic roses,
A rose red brick house where twins lived.
Their father called one "Pete", the other "Twin".
    For "Hey Twin!" he would shout.

Down the street came a giant man dressed old
With a clock in his belly: I dreamt that.   30
Babies of six months in their christening shrouds
Reach out for me by the ding dong church yard
    Which stands on the hill above the dam.

■ ELEVENTH LETTER

Shakespearean Gardens

The Tempest   The violet lightning of a March thunderstorm glaring the patches of ice still stuck to the streets.

Two Gentlemen of Verona   On Wellington St. an elegant colonel-looking gentleman with waxed white moustachioes that came to tight little points.

Merry Wives of Windsor   The Ladies' Auxiliary of the Orange Lodge marched down the street in white dresses with orange bows on them.

Richard III   At last all the children ran away from home and were brought up by an old spinster who lived down the street.

Henry VIII   Mr. White's second wife was the first Mrs. Brown and the first Mrs. White was the second Mrs. Brown.

Troilus & Cressida   "Well, I haven't been to that old Festival yet but since it began I've had ten different boyfriends."

Titus Andronicus   Young Mr. Wood to-day lost his right hand in an accident at the lumber yards.

Romeo & Juliet   Romeo & Juliet Streets.

Timon of Athens   Old Miss Shipman lived alone in a weatherbeaten old cottage and could occasionally be seen out on the front lawn cutting the grass with a small sickle.

228

Julius Caesar   Antony wore a wrist watch in the Normal School production although he never looked at it during the oration.

Macbeth   Principal Burdoch's often expressed opinion was that a great many people would kill a great many other people if they knew for certain they could get away with it.

Hamlet   A girl at the bakery took out a boat on the river, tied candlesticks to her wrists and drowned herself.

King Lear   Mr. Upas was a silver haired cranky old individual who complained that the meat was too tough at the boarding house.

Othello   At the edge of town there stood a lonely white frame building—a deserted Negro church.

The Merchant of Venice   When my cousin worked for the Silversteins she had her own private roll of baloney kept aside in the refrigerator for her.

Henry V   The local armouries are made of the usual red brick with the usual limestone machicolation.

■ *TWELFTH LETTER*

The Bicycle

Halfway between childhood & manhood,
    More than a hoop but never a car,
The bicycle talks gravel and rain pavement
    On the highway where the dead frogs are.

Like sharkfish the cars blur by,
    Filled with the two-backed beast
One dreams of, yet knows not the word for,
    The accumulating sexual yeast.

Past the house where the bees winter,
    I climb on the stairs of my pedals   10
To school murmuring irregular verbs
    Past the lion with legs like a table's.

Autumn blows the windfalls down
    With a twilight horn of dead leaves.
I pick them up in the fence of November
    And burs on my sweater sleeves.

229

Where a secret robin is wintering
  By the lake in the fir grove dark
Through the fresh new snow we stumble
  That Winter has whistled sharp.   *20*

The March wind blows me ruts over,
  Puddles past, under red maple buds,
Over culvert of streamling, under
  White clouds and beside bluebirds.

Fireflies tell their blinking player
  Piano hesitant tales
Down at the bridge through the swamp
  Where the ogre clips his rusty nails.

Between the highschool & the farmhouse
  In the country and the town   *30*
It was a world of love and of feeling
  Continually floating down

On a soul whose only knowledge
  Was that everything was something,
This was like that, that was like this—
  In short, everything was
  The bicycle of which I sing.

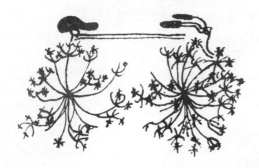

7 THE DANCE OF DEATH AT LONDON, ONTARIO – 1963

Invitation to a Dance

Blow the trumpet! Beat the drum!
  This town's a dance of death.
Did you think you could not come?
  You'll dance when you're out of breath.

What is the tune the traffic plays?
  It's my exhausted pipe
Playing my shambling mazurkas,
  Humming my sideswipe.

At Springbank I toot the lurch.
  Your footstep's the armoury echo.   10
The skyscrape lights up my search.
  Cathedrals cross my shadow.

I take all the undertakers,
  I gnash my teeth at the cenotaph.
Of all differences I'm the raker
  Together, and levelly laugh

Down Winery Hill up to Arva.
  Horton Street I equal to Regent,
Infesting all flesh with my skeleton larva
And so—click clack—behold! my dancing regiment!   20

Executive Esquire & Grocery Boy
Man, Woman, Doctor, Child, Bishop
The Scavenger & the Rich Young Lady
    Painter & Poet & Cop

235

The Executive

   I walk back from the club to the office
Though Queens Ave knows the weight of my Rolls Royce.
   Life Insurance ensures my assurance.
At this moment five girls type my voice.

Death

   Hey! Where do you think you're going?
I need you to type out my deeds.
   I've a nice tidy room where you'll work
Though the ribbon is tangled with weeds.

The Clergyman

PRIEST: I often think as I drink tea
    Of Faith & Hope & Charity.
MINISTER: I'm sure that Faith, Hope & Charity
    Oft think of us as we drink tea.

Death

Shepherds, the morning sky is red.
    I've found half of thy charge.
Whatever thy task was, find it out,
    For I'm near and much at large.

The Rich Young Lady

My father breaks hundreds of bonds,
   My mother subscribes to *The Queen*,
I spent last winter in Antigua,
   Our swimming pool's drinkably clean.

Death

Then come ride with me & my hounds
   Or if you wish to this car keep,
And we'll drive with the speed of the wind
   To my park where the shadows are deep.

The Open Line

SHE: Uh—that man who just phoned uh was right
    Uh if they uh cut down all the trees—
HE: Yes, madam. You've a very good point there.
    Then the cars wouldn't slip on the wet leaves?

Death

My talkative lady crunch! snap!
    How pale you are holding your phone.
You should get outside more & you will
    Beneath the dead leaves all alone.

The Policeman

At Colonel Talbot's courtly house
   I hanged the rebels rash, sir.
To-day I'm herdsman of the cars
   But once used the public lash, sir.

Death

I cannot see you wherever you are
   But I feel you weigh down my pan
That dips down and scoops up you both—
   Courthouse & policeman.

The Bride & The Bridegroom

SHE: Mother & father have spared no expense.
　　Is that someone's foot on my train?
HE: I bet I remember this moment
　　Again & again & again.

Death

There go the bride & the bridegroom!
　　They'll stay at our hostelry.
To its luscious bridal chamber
　　We've devised an ancient key.

The Grocery Boy

At the corner of Richmond & Talbot Street,
  Oranges, cornflakes cellophane & ham,
I fill up the bags & the boxes.
  Is that black car the one you mean, m'am?

Death

Long enough have you drudged for the stomach!
  Drop that box at your feet in this parking lot!
It's just dust that I need for my supper.
  Put yourself in this box that I've got.

The Child

On Dawnview Ave I live.
  Our sidewalk's just put in.
I play outside till it's Cartoon Time
  Or sometime's Rin-Tin-Tin.

Death

My hoop is Time which I drive on
  Quicker than you can, my boy.
  I drive it down this street to-day
Since you are now my newest toy.

The Scavenger

Down Rectory Street one grizzly gray day
   I pulled my little one horse dray
Filled with rejected, broken things
   When I heard & felt a voice that stings.

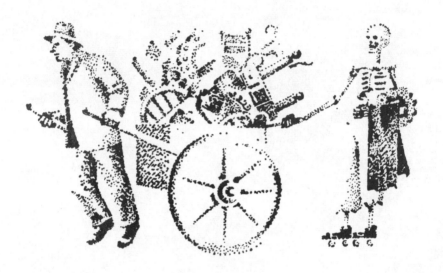

Death

At the bottom of the city's pit
   You carried off things I'd sawed free.
Now I'd like to have them back
   And you to come & dance with me.

The Poet

Since I write you I well know
   What you will doubtless say
That every word I write must go
   The dusty change of vowel way.

Death

Of course. All your tropes and iambics
   Become my leaden fiddlesticks.
My laurel soon will make you dull,
   And your tongue dust pepper in your skull.

The Painter

Eye am the I of the world.
  I ravish the unravishable bride.
Infernoes & Sunday Mornings
  I produce with pardonable pride.

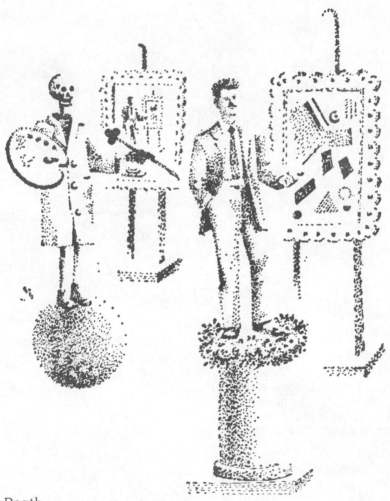

Death

My brush is never half so fine.
  In fact it's a three-pronged club.
Although you've made my visage thine
  I now will thy skull engrave & rub.

The Doctor

At the very gates of life I
  Allow the human vine.
Nurse, take away this little cup.
  I've filled it full of wine.

Death

Yes, give me that cup and I
  Will spill it some time, some place.
Shall I carry it safe for years of miles
  Or fling it now into your face?

249

Conclusio

Now that this tottery dance has begun
    Is not your life seen a tower of burs,
Its vertebrae steps wet with foul Thames water,
    The key in your fork & shut with a curse?

Each night the king of this tower comes down
    To see who has left the latest brat
Whom he lifts abruptly, a juicy foundling,
    And just in time for look—a rat!

Up the burry brambly rackety stairs
    Of gurgly Clarence & Montsarrat Ave—
'What my child would you like to be?
    See them dancing hand in hand to the grave?

Would you like to be Esquire or Grocery Boy?
    Man, Woman, Doctor, Child, Bishop?
A Scavenger or a Rich Young Lady?
    A Painter, a Poet or a Cop?'

Like a wee windmill the little brown bat flew away.
With its blue light the Snow Truck turned into Spook Street.
Then the baby replied to the King of the Tower who now
At the top changed to an Angel of Death moth with written wings

'Death's Head Moth, King of the Tower of Burs
    With streets and avenues written on your wings,
I shall come to London and join your dancing.
    I will be one of your things,

Yet stand not in dread of you,
    Thy tumble drum, nor thy hollow fife.
For I know a Holy One who some day will
    Shut up thy book with the hands of Life.'

250

8 TWO CHAPTERS FROM AN EMBLEM BOOK 1969-70

THE CASTLE

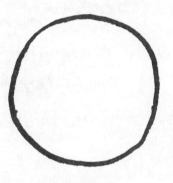

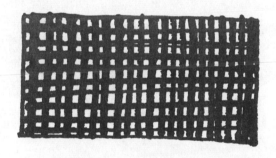

This is the ground plan
For a castle called Man

There was a farm
       divided in two
½ of it surly
       brickmaker
              owned
swale & slough
       clay &
              stiff
I nto this from the
              western half

Jutted an orchard of 50
                    young trees

Captain Grape Arbour &
              Major Mulberry
Angel greening trees
              in whitewashed trunks

Roods & perches fought clayhole &
                              swamp

& the lawns won, the gravel pit's
                              gone
       Now the farm's one.

THE FARM

254

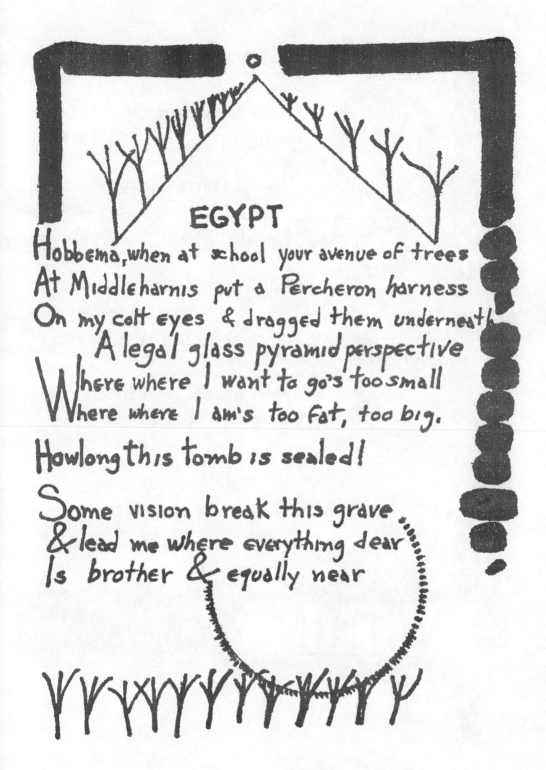

EGYPT

Hobbema, when at school your avenue of trees
At Middleharnis put a Percheron harness
On my colt eyes & dragged them underneath
     A legal glass pyramid perspective
Where where I want to go's too small
Where where I am's too fat, too big.

How long this tomb is sealed!

Some vision break this grave
  & lead me where everything dear
Is brother & equally near

In man's eye a tear
        reflecting
In a fish
        a face looks out
The twilight elms along the fence
Huge cows, a mouse, green
        horses seem
This crystal holds a mineral
        fern
Clouds, clouds you
        build for me
Architectural
        afternoons
WHERE in those clouds
        are men &
In their eyes...

WITHIN WITHIN

256

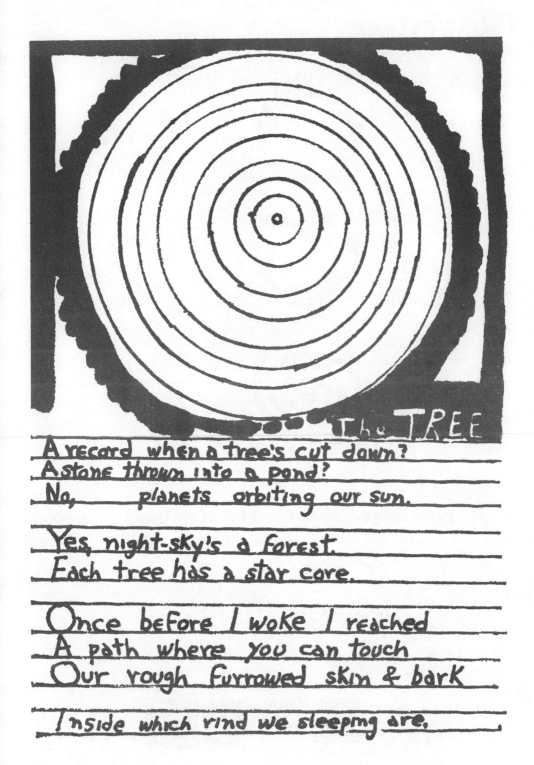

The TREE

A record when a tree's cut down?
A stone thrown into a pond?
No,   planets orbiting our sun.

Yes, night-sky's a forest.
Each tree has a star core.

Once before I woke I reached
A path where you can touch
Our rough furrowed skin & bark

Inside which rind we sleeping are.

A one man band? Understand
& you can
This is a Man

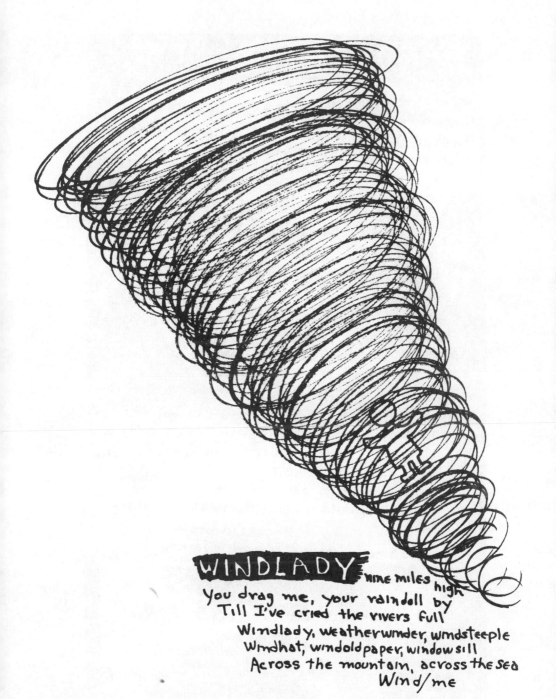

WINDLADY nine miles high
You drag me, your raindoll by
Till I've cried the rivers full
Windlady, weatherwinder, windsteeple
Windhat, windoldpaper, windowsill
Across the mountain, across the sea
Wind/me

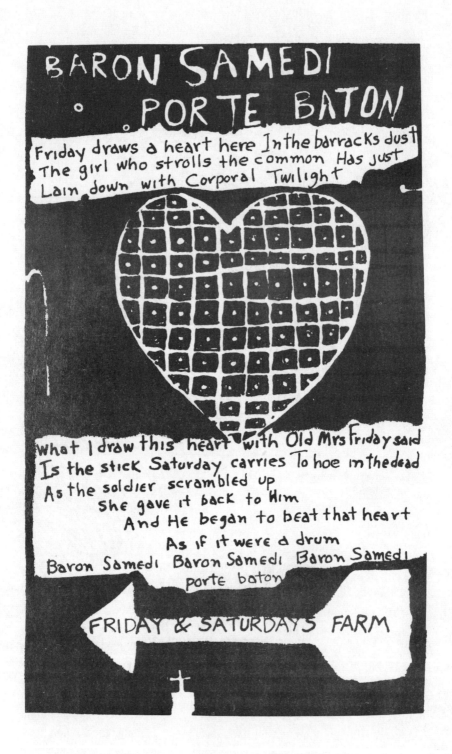

BARON SAMEDI
PORTE BATON

Friday draws a heart here In the barracks dust
The girl who strolls the common Has just
Lain down with Corporal Twilight

What I draw this heart with Old Mrs Friday said
Is the stick Saturday carries To hoe in the dead
As the soldier scrambled up
        She gave it back to Him
            And He began to beat that heart
            As if it were a drum
Baron Samedi   Baron Samedi   Baron Samedi
            porte baton

FRIDAY & SATURDAYS FARM

When the clouds cross the sky

Ride thro' the stars   6 brothers late for supper
BRAVE   MESSENGER   **STRONG**
Clerk   Worthless   Bad

At the last house one table for their elbows
Beneath—a cellar where all lost things are
And where the clouds are kept at night
Elm tree, drive in the late ones past my moon

Brother   Wife   Husband
children   children   children

What thunder shakes the windowpane
Run out & see who's coming down the lane

THE LAST HOUSE

261

THE HAT

Against me wears the wind a coat
And to protect her from your feet
Ma Earth puts on a dusty shoe
Rain against him taps a roof
Against me puts the Sun a hat

Hey you! Tramp! When is it that
You'll take off your dusty shoes
& hang up your coat & hat

Child, listen: that will be
When in my tramping, weeping, searching

I have found   A river to the sea.

9 SOME DRAMATIC VERSE 1953-71

From "Night-Blooming Cereus":
  A Domestic Song-Cycle

[Mrs. Brown's kitchen: a very crowded place, but in a small two-room cottage everything gets mixed in together—parlor and kitchen. Mrs. Brown has just finished her supper, and after taking a last sip of tea folds her hands for an after-dinner blessing.]

A Blessing

    My Lord I thank for bread and meat
    You give more bread than I can cut
    More for to drink than I can cup
    More to myself than I can eat.

    These pitchers and these platters hold
    The milk and honey of thy love
    And I am grateful for thy grace
    As starving prophet was of old.

    But in between my praying hands
    And in between my fast shut eyes   10
    The table of thy manna stands
    From whose delight may I not rise. Amen.

[She gets up and begins to clear up the dishes, shaking out the tablecloth, going to the stove for hot water and dishpan.]

Washing Dishes

    Now I will gather up and wash the dishes,
    Plate cup knife fork spoon and jug.
    Now will my plate and cup be just like fishes.
    There used to be so many more to gather up.

    Even I an old woman have servants and children,
    Plate cup fork knife jug and spoon.
    Unlike children away they cannot run,
    Safe on the shelves of the cupboard in this room.

    I suppose we are his china and cutlery,
    Plate cup jug spoon fork and knife.   10
    He washes us when we Him see.
    Easier to wash these than wash a life.

But when I the old woman am taken from the table,
Cup fork knife spoon jug and plate
If they are not broken, before I break, will
Faithful remain behind to demonstrate

To others who may own them after,
Plate cup knife spoon jug and fork,
Daily to baptize themselves in the water
Of thinking how they can for Heaven work.   20

[The dishes are put away, the cupboard door closed, the dishwater somehow disposed of. She gets the broom from behind the door.]

Sweeping

Look at the faces on the floor
In the wood of the boards they are
Faces of dust I sweep with a broom,
Sweeping the dust in this room.
Sweeping sweeping sweeping sweeping
Has a sound like weeping.
If I kept all the dust I've swept
It would be she I have wept
Whose face appears more often than not
In the dust and the fire and the knot   10
And the blowing rain on the window
And the tree-branches' shadow
Contain your face there! and again there!
My lost girl in the dust in the air.
But it is best to go on sweeping
Over the faces better than weeping.
Here is the face of an old man peeping.
Here is the face of a young man reaping.
Here is the face of an old woman sweeping.

[A bit tired with so much activity, she sits in the rocking chair.]

Rocking

Rocking rocking rocking rocking
Very very slowly.
What I have been doing rocking,
Most of my life lately.

Sewing at a shirt or stocking
As quickly as I can
And what the people to me bring
I sew at while rocking.

Like selling footsteps to all houses
My stitches go through cloth   10
Of caps and nightgowns and blouses
Dresses handkerchiefs and vests.

I sew for everyone here,
I the restless stillness,
My thread looks through cloth for tear
And the butcher's apron.

The sewing connects each one
To myself except for her.
She walks about beneath the sun
Without my sewing snow.   20

As the white snow fills fields and lanes
Till they cover me all,
Upon my old and long-used bones
Rocking and sewing fall.

[Mrs. Brown gets up and begins to move the plants away from the
windows. She brings them to the table. The Night Blooming Cereus, on a
special stand, is moved to a central position.]

A Plant Song

The night
Comes now with its frost
In which a flower is lost
Unless from windowsill
Their keeper keep them day until.

Patience Plant
Come here now
To this table
And Elephant Ear
The frost to get you won't be able.   10

Christmas Cactus
Busy Lizzie too
Red geraniums
And the farthest Wandering Jew.

Night Blooming Cereus
Night Blooming Cereus
Now for us
You will come out
After a century
To see my friends and me.   20

Dark green
Dark green, dark green,
Your leaves, your leaves
As time without
Her being seen,
The years her mother sadly grieves.

Within
Your blossom may I see
Within the leaves of grief
The face of my lost girl   *30*
Or if that is not to be
May somehow lighter be my sheaf.

[*She sits at the harmonium, finds her place in the hymn-book, and sings
to her own accompaniment.*]

A Hymn

Our Lord has prepared for us
Houses in Heaven.
How many rooms have they?
They number seven.
And what will we do
In this Heavenly House?
Watch flowers come out
All the day through.

In his cellar you'll find
Cool milk and sweet wine   *10*
And those so inclined
May spend all the day there.
And what will we do
In this Heavenly House?
Whatever you want to
All the day through.

In the woodshed you'll notice
Trees chopped up ready
And fine dry split kindling
For fires all so steady,   *20*
And what will we do
In this Heavenly House?
Watch the fire burn
All the day through.

In the pantry you'll find loaves
That ravens have brought,
Loaves everlasting
All fresh and hot.
Our Lord has prepared for us
Houses in Heaven   30
With tables of wheat bread
Spiritually leavened.

In his parlor the carpets
Refresh tired feet
Like valleys of green grass
All dewy and sweet.
And what will we do
In this Heavenly House?
Always be visiting
All the day through.   40

And up in the bedroom
Four angels are bedposts
Who each with a gold broom
Sweep care from your eyes.
Oh what will we do
In this Heavenly House—
Dreaming true dreamings
All the day through.

And in the seventh room should be
A pair of folded hands   50
Praising him who built for thee
A house that ever stands.
All children and cousins
All brothers and sisters
And fathers and mothers
And relatives lost,
Lost loved ones
Dear faces
Will be with you there
If not here, there.   60

[A knock at the door]

1953

From "The Killdeer" (second version), Act II :
*   The River of Time*

[The scene is the late Mrs. Gardner's deserted cottage. The two old women are cleaning up.]

Mrs. Budge
    Oh, the river of time, the river of time,
    The clouds of the moments, the clouds of the moments,
    Clouds of escaping birds from the dark barn.
    I grab here, I grab there, birds you escape me.
    The wind of the hours, wind of the hours,
    The snow of the minutes, snow of the minutes,
    It all falls into the river of time and is swept away.

Mrs. Delta
    Oh, the river of time, the river of time.

Mrs. Budge
    What am I to dust now? Those curlicues
    On the stove? No, you couldn't have done them,   **10**
    Mrs. Delta, I could plant them with seeds.
    Just look, Mrs. Delta.

Mrs. Delta
    I ain't done nothing but mop round that stove,
    Mrs. Budge. I mopped, and I mop.

1960, 1968

From a version of Euripides' "Bacchae"
    Act I : The Earthquake Chorus

Chorus
> Oh barley! Barley, barley, barley! John Barleycorn!
> Where have you vanished? Where have you gone?
>
> Wild grape! Little grape I miss you! Miss you from my fence.
> Why have you fled? Who has driven you hence?
>
> Tanager! Red bird! Heart heart of the green bush.
> You never sing now in the cold still hush.

[They make sounds like the autumn wind.]

> In your prison/Dionysos/Can you hear us?
>
> Who has kidnapped all the barley I shall tell.
> With a scythe of cold wind and rain has the fall.
>
> But the barley and the grape, they are hidden safe away.   10
> The grape in the cellar and the barley in the barn—
>
> Where they
>
> While the wind sings with a cold narrow mouth
> Yet the red bird still sings in the warm far south—
>
> Where they
>
> In the cask and the mow and far away –
>
> In your prison/Dionysos/Can you hear us?
>
> Fall and winter, fall and winter
> Low dark sky of bristling rain
> Fall and winter leaf and seed imprison   20
>
> The North Wind blows through branches bare
> Frozen the ground and sharp the hail
> Over the seed and the nut's dark jail

The world lies asleep in a jail of snow
Ice chains the river, no birds in the sky
      King Pentheus
In your winter we die.

But the barley and the grape, they are hidden safe away,
The grape in a bottle, the barley in a barn

      Where they   30

Dionysus [*singing in prison*]
      Where I!
      Wait out patiently
      The grave granary
      The cobweb cellar night
      Where they
      Where I
      Await the spring of light
      The cock crow cry
      When once again the day
      Is mine   40
      Is thine
      Run shadows!
      For the sun returns
      And burns
      Up the darkness

      The Sun comes marching to the North
      And beats his ice armour with a forth
      Flinging mace of fire!

      In my jail I shout I am the son
      Of Earth and of Heaven. Our loved one -   50
      Where is he whom we desire?

      I lie in the cold dark earth in chains
      We search for you with love like rain
      I break my bonds! I break!

      Oh Sun & leaf & rain & bud take breath
      Thrust up through the pavements of King Death
      And! Shake King Winter - Castle - shake!

      I break the earth with a seedling storm
      I come with a storm not of wind but of stone
            Our lord comes!   60

[*They shudder & topple down as the earth quakes. They are watching Pentheus' castle topple to the ground.*]

> The towers and spires of this king's castle
> Search the ground to hide their crowns.
> The idol of Winter comes tumbling down.

[*Dionysos enters as fresh as ever. He revives them, lifts them up. He snaps asunder his chain. From moment to moment there are further quake sounds from off stage.*]

> There! Do not fear!
> I am he
> Who deathlessly
> The Spring of Spring
> Now brings
> To thee!

Act II : Agave's lament and the ending

Agave
  Where is the rest of my son?
Cadmus
  We have gathered him up.

[*The guards come forward with a heavy basket made of reeds which they set down in front of Agave and Cadmus.*]

Agave [*an ominous humming off stage*]
  My son, How I have torn you.
  Who bore you, grew you in my side
  I laughed at the unseen, unbelievable
  And he -- that dread god -- made
  Unbeget, uncreate, give life, then destroy
  Fill a cradle with nettles and thorns and knives
  And wean my child on his own blood.
  I cannot bear the sentence: to murder that I mothered   10
  To stand before my son a mangled puzzle --

[*Dionysos' entry cuts her short. She and Cadmus crouch by the basket. Dionysos takes down Pentheus' head and holds it up. He and the chorus look down on Agave and Cadmus.*]

273

Dionysos
    What comes first? To believe upon me,
    Believe in my father a bridegroom of fire
    Believe in his child who was torn for you.
    I died for your joy. I am torn each day.
    Tear me, mock me and I shall tear you.

[as they sing Dionysos takes down the severed head]

Chorus
    Have faith that the dark ground
        Is sown with green grass
    Believe that the drowned man
        Shall turn to spring rain   20
    Know that the wild wind
        Can whistle a song.

Dionysos [holds up the head which sings]
    And sing my child, Pentheus.
    The dreadful lantern of your head
    Shall well forth in a hymn of light.

Pentheus
    I believe
Chorus
    In the dark ground
Pentheus
    I grieve
Chorus
    Too late you found
Pentheus
    I leave   30
Chorus
    With joy thy soul does run
Pentheus
    I perceive
Chorus
    The sacred shadow of the sun.
Dionysos and Chorus
    Behold! the wonder Dionysos brings
    Death into life, a severed head that sings!

1963

From the Radio Collage "Canada Dash, Canada Dot"
    Part II : The Line Up and Down

Yonge Street

Man
  Existence waked me here on this cement tapeworm
    Called Yonge Street
  Take a step, take a breath, take a step, take a breath
    This day and every day
    Called Yonge Street
  I can remember the tokens that made it all go
    Eliza Regina Imperatrix
  It was a sort of weather in your pocket
  I can remember a fishhead at Savarin's Grill
  The crowds of other-me's walked above the rush   10
  Beneath them lakeward of their own sewerage

Girl
  By the way, where is the golden branch I gave you?

Man
  A cunning Melinda Street boss ate it like a candy stick
  He wore a gray suit and had bellies under his eyes.

Girl
  And where is the silver cup and grail we gave you?
Man
  A paper King Street woman with instalments for eyes
  And typewriters for feet—she pawned it.
  But I have here instead this long gray vertebrae
  The backbone of a city; my backbone as a matter of fact.
  Now that I'm dead   20
  Will it do instead
  Of the golden branch and the silver cup
  I was given when
  First I journeyed to the world of men?

1958, 1966

275

From "Listen to the Wind", Act II
  "Lock up your doors and pen your flocks"

Chorus
  Lock up your doors and pen your flocks,
    A storm comes with the night,
  The stars go out and the windows latch,
    Babies cry out in fright.

  Over the hills and under the sky
    The huntsman and his hounds,
  The huntsman's dark and 12 feet high —
    Hear him galloping by.

  His dogs gnash in their kennels of skull
    And now he lets them out,   10
  His dogs of rage and his wolves of blood
    Raise a dreadful shout

  Over the hills and under the sky
    The huntsman and his hounds.
  He rides the wind with a dreadful cry
    And Hell itself comes nigh.

  Closer they come. Have you shut the door?
    What have you left outside,
  His horse must eat. Leave out a thing.
    He will not be denied.   20

  Over the hills and under the sky
    The huntsman and his hounds —
  "Have you blood for us and any bones?"
    Hear their thrilling cry!

  We've left a last sheaf in the field.
    Huntsman it is for you.
  Take it and leave ourselves unharmed.
    And do not us pursue.

  Over the hills and under the sky
    Over the hills and under the sky   30
      Over the hills and under the sky
        Over the hills and under the sky.

1966

276

From "Colours in the Dark", two "pyramids" :
    Scene 8 : Berry Picking

[*Bear runs off with child, kids enter shrieking*]

Kids
    A bear ran off with Sadie! A bear ran off with
    Sadie! And it takes a lot of people to produce
    one child.

[*They form a family tree pyramid with a reappearing Sadie.*]

Kids
It takes
Two parents
Four Grandparents
Eight Great grandparents
Sixteen Great great grandparents
Thirty-two Great great great grandparents
Sixty-four Great great great great grandparents   10
One hundred and twenty-eight Great great great great great
grandparents
Two hundred and fifty-six Great great great great great great
grandparents
Five hundred and twelve Great great great great great great
great grandparents
One thousand and twenty-four Great great great great great great
great great grandparents

[*It would take over a thousand people to do this scene: at Listeners'
Workshop we did it with thirty-two people: the children here
suggested—by a triangle arrangement, the thousand ancestors behind
each human being. Have one group of players in charge of chanting
"Great great" & "grandparents".*]

Sadie
    Are you there 1,024 ancestors?

[*a feeble rustle*]

    Are you there 512
    Are you there 256
    Are you there 128

[*sound gets louder, less ghost-like and more human*]

    Are you there 64
    Are you there 32   20
    Are you there 16

277

[More recent ancestors step forward and say firmly and clearly what we have only dimly heard: "We're here."]

Are you there 8
Are you there 4
Are you there Mother and Father?

[Gramp, Ma and Pa step forward and establish the next scene as the kids fade away.]

Scene 21 : The Bridge

... OR EVEN ADOLF HITLER HAD 1024 GREAT GREAT GREAT GREAT GREAT GREAT GREAT GREAT GRANDPARENTS AND KEPT A PLAY BOX TOO.

[Father speaks, Son acts out situation for him.]

Pa
On one of my walks—I came to a river. There
was a bridge. But under the bridge there was
a swan. He hissed at me. I couldn't cross.

[Set this up as a bridge with something white under it. A girl with long white glove as the swan's neck. The situation—the entire company crosses the bridge, but the hero can't. On the other side they beckon to him silently, but he won't cross.]

I can't cross. I'm afraid! I was like one of
those people you hear about in mental hospitals
Who can't go through a doorway.

The pebble is a huge dark hill I must climb   10
The dewdrop is a great storm lake that we must cross
The string is a road that I cannot find
The straw is a sign whose meaning I forget
　　　　Hill　　　Lake　　　Road　　　Sign

[The Bear chases him to the middle of the bridge. A tug of war between the people and the Bear helped by Lady Death. He is pulled across—perhaps loses something. The Bear and Lady Death dispute over this—with some other sinister figures who gather. Lady Death is played by Grandmother. They fade and the cast form the family tree pyramid; the Stage turns slowly yellow.]

All

                    It Takes
              The Remembering
          Of   four   seasons
        Eight   Stars
      Sixteen   Sunsets
    Thirty-Two   Wind whistles   *20*
  Sixty-four   Dewdrops in the sunrise
One hundred and twenty-eight   Trembling leaves
  Two hundred and fifty-six   Pebbles
    Five hundred and twelve   Snowflakes
  One thousand and twenty-four   Cloud shadows
              To make one soul

[*The family tree pyramid now reverses so it is an arrow pointing at a
child standing on the trestles. This child turns his face. He is masked
and dressed as Adolf Hitler.*
SCREEN: Swastika.
*We hear a Nazi children's song and the roar of a Nuremberg rally. All
file off, Father helping the Hitler boy down and off.*]

1967

From "Donnelly", Act I:
   The case against Donnelly,
   and Jennie's dawn-song at the wake

[The scene is the wake for the Donnellys. We shift back and forth in time as Mrs. Donnelly tells her son Will about their troubles, and the grown-up Jennie and Will comment on what happened. The "clappers" are the Donnelly's friends, the "stampers" their enemies.]

Mrs. Donnelly
   One night, Will, your father was up the road visiting a farmer he was to do some work for the next morning. They followed him there.
Stampers
   Come out Jim Donnelly
Mrs. Donnelly
   They said to your father.
First Stamper
   Put on you my good fellow and come out till two or three of your neighbours that wish you well gets a sight of your purty face you babe of grace.
Mrs. Donnelly
   Your father kept quiet. So they say.
Stampers
   Open up in the Queen's name, Jim Donnelly. We've a warrant for your arrest.
Mrs. Donnelly
   Your father stood behind the door and he says
Mr. Donnelly
   Who are you that wants me at all.
Mrs. Donnelly
   and they says
Stampers
   Come out first avourneen.
Mrs. Donnelly
   He opened the door and came out.
Stampers
   Jim Donnelly. The Whitefeet hear that you let one of your mares stand to Sealey's entire horse last Monday coming home from the fair.
Mrs. Donnelly
   To which your father replied

280

Mr. Donnelly
    [*at back stage where the crowd has been focussing*] It was love at
    first sight. Shure Sealey's stallion was mounting my one mare before I
    could stop him. I had my back turned at the time just for the merest
    minute getting my other mare's tail disentangled from a thornbush.
Stampers
    Did you not know no Whitefoot is to have any dealings with the
    Protestant and the heretic Sealey?
Mr. Donnelly
    Yes, but it was
Stampers
    Kneel, Donnelly. Get down on your knees.

[*But he stands. A barrel is rolled back and forth a bit in the crowd.*]

First Stamper
    Swear [*striking a book*] that you will not withdraw yourself from this
    society — the Whitefeet [*candles*].
Mr. Donnelly
    But you see I won't kneel. And I won't swear.
Second Stamper
    If you refuse [*the barrel is rolled around*] if you refuse, Donnelly, you
    won't know the day nor the hour nor the [*light stamping rhythm
    repeated*]
Mr. Donnelly
    No, I'm not.
First Stamper
    Kneel.
Mr. Donnelly
    No.
First Stamper
    Swear.
Mr. Donnelly
    No! I won't kneel.
Mrs. Donnelly
    So they cursed your father and called him a
All
    Blackfoot!

281

[*The barrel is rolled off to some secret end.*]

Mrs. Donnelly
    Isn't today your birthday Will? Go over to that old tree the storm fell
    down and see what you find hidden in among the roots.
The Boy Will
    A fiddle. Is it for my birthday, Mother?
Mrs. Donnelly
    It's for your life, Will. Anybody that talks of Whitefeet and Blackfeet
    in Canada here is nothing but bullies and blowhards. We showed
    them in Ireland and we'll show them here in Canada. What does your
    father care if they've followed him. After the harvest he'll own this
    ground we stand on and the fields he's made. You'll see — they'll try
    to drive us off, Will.
All
    A high gray hill   That's Keeper's Hill   ash trees
Mrs. Donnelly
    But here we'll stay
All
    Thorn tree   blackbird flying close   far
    farther   farthest   away
Mrs. Donnelly
    If you're afraid you should be
Stampers
    Ireland
Mrs. Donnelly
    If you're not   you'll live
Clappers
    Ireland
Mrs. Donnelly
    Ireland. Old names — Blackfoot! Whitefoot! Slavery.
    Canada's a new fiddle, Will, and we're free.
Stampers
    [*softly as the mother and son mingle with the chorus*]   Ireland
Jennie
    And that is why, mother, they burnt you
Clappers
    First with their tongues

Jennie
                    then with their kerosene
   Because you were tall, you were different
                    and you weren't afraid
   Be not afraid now at the thorn apple fields
Stampers
   Stars above   clouds below   and snow still around
   Mourning till dawn   from midnight to dawn
   A bone for Jennie   and a fiddle for Will
   Four stones where there once was a home
   Five dead people have come to this house
Jennie
   I help my mother cross the thorn apple fields
   We pay you toll with our thoughts and tears
The Man Will
   Requiem aeternam dona eis, Domine, et lux perpetua luceat eis.
Jennie
   Cum sanctus tuis in aeternum, quia pius es
The Man Will
   For at dawn comes a sleigh
Jennie
   To bear you away
   For awhile from us
   As we mourn in this house
   The last tollgate before harvest and heaven.

1971

INDEX TO TITLES

INDEX
TO FIRST LINES

About this Book

The text in this edition was photo-composed using Compugraphic 11 pt. Mallard, titles were handset in 14 pt. Goudy Old Style medium italic and major heads were handset in century-old wood type owned by Corey Herrington, whose firm (Herrington Printing and Publishing of Erin, Ontario) also set the text.

Reproduction proofs of all titling were drawn by hand on a press once the property of James Reaney's *Alphabet* magazine.

The paper is Byronic text (white) brocade finish (130m on 25" x 38" basis).

This book was designed and printed offset on Multilith equipment by Tim Inkster and Mike McDonald at Press Porcépic of Erin, Ontario.